PROJECT-BASED HOMESCHOOLING

MENTORING SELF-DIRECTED LEARNERS

PROJECT-BASED HOMESCHOOLING

MENTORING
SELF-DIRECTED
LEARNERS

Lori McWilliam Pickert

Dedicated to my sons
Dominic and Jack Henry

and to my first collaborators
Chris, Jackie, Leisa, Andrea, and Emily

Table of Contents

There are two aspects of providing occasions for wonderful ideas. One is being prepared to accept children's ideas. The other is providing a setting which suggests wonderful ideas to children. — Eleanor Duckworth

Introduction

This book is not a recipe for how to homeschool that you can confidently follow to bake up a nice loaf of educated child.

It's not a purist approach that requires you to follow it to the letter, memorize its fight song, and clash antlers with anyone who is doing it slightly differently than you.

Instead, it's a collection of strategies for helping children direct and manage their own learning.

I had an unpleasant public-school experience followed by an uninspiring college experience, so when it came to my own children, I edged toward the whole subject of education somewhat warily. I started by opening a private school — my own idealized school with art studios for each classroom and a curriculum based on long-term, child-led projects. It was lovely. It was unsustainable. I believe it was John Holt who once pointed out that most wonderful schools are built around one strong personality and when that personality leaves, the school tends to fall apart. After several years, I was a tired wizard, weary of maintaining my magical school by dint of continuous, 24/7/365 spell-weaving.

I segued right into homeschooling with the exact same values about what and how childen should learn, and it was a vacation to be in charge of two children rather than several dozen. My younger child wasn't yet five; my firstborn, a few years older, was already an old hat at directing and managing his own learning. It was an easy transition.

But homeschooling has its own challenges. Every homeschooling parent is a kind of wizard, having to conjure up a network of friends (for yourself as well as your child), learning experiences (ditto), books, movies, science experiments, nature walks, arts and crafts, play dates, and petting-zoo visits, and weave it all together with three meals a day (not to mention snacks), toys, more books, pets, more arts and crafts, more friends, and etc., because homeschooling isn't just education, it's an entire lifestyle. It starts when you decide to begin and it never lets up, ever.

When I was running my tiny private school, I also worked as an educational consultant, traveling around and giving workshops, presenting at conferences, and training and mentoring teachers. I got a very interesting, inside view of how schools work and how difficult it is to exact real and lasting change. Whether you're a parent, a teacher, or an administrator, the system is so solidly built on a certain set of ideas that it's almost impossible for one person to get things moving in a different direction. Instead, the person championing change becomes that one strong personality, the wizard who conjures up a wonderful classroom or a brief Camelot of a school. Alas, the magic can't seem to last. That one classroom is a brief stop for children — one really wonderful year — between more ordinary classrooms. The children move on. The teacher becomes discouraged, the school closes, or the administration changes. The wizards leave and take the magic with them.

Homeschooling/unschooling parents, by comparison, have much more freedom and control. They can maintain the same goals and focus on the same values year after year. They can learn from their mistakes and try again *right away*. They can capitalize on their successes *immediately*. They can discard what doesn't work and try something else, without needing permission from a committee or a boss, without waiting until next semester or next year. They can accumulate their wisdom — perhaps slowly, but isn't that how wisdom usually comes? — and use it without delay. They can stay with an idea for a long time and gain authentic understanding and real expertise — which is the essence of project-based homeschooling.

This book posits a simple idea — that children need the opportunity to direct and manage their own learning — and then suggests ways that we adults can help them do that. All of these suggestions may not work for you; some of them, you may already be doing. It's not a blueprint. If you find an idea that appeals to you, you can go from there. You can adapt it to what you already know about your child and your family life. This is how project-based homeschooling works: you start from where you are, today, and you explore what interests you.

When I was working as an educational consultant, I had this experience several times: I was brought into a school by the administrators. They wanted very much to embrace new values for how their students should learn. They wanted the children's education to be interest-led, to move at a natural pace, to be mentored and facilitated thoughtfully. They wanted to toss out the old way of doing things and embrace these new methods *right away*, immediately, without delay.

Therefore, they wanted the teachers to be trained in how to change the curriculum, remake their classrooms, and start working with children in an entirely new way *right away*, immediately, without delay. They wanted their staff to toss out their old routines and materials, move the furniture, redecorate their classrooms, toss their old lesson plans, and do everything differently — right away, immediately, without delay.

Many times, the administrators (excited and inspired by new ideas, motivated to give their students a better learning experience and a more wonderful school as soon as possible) would miss the fact that they were championing holistic learning for the students *but not for the teachers*. The adults didn't get to learn at their own pace — they were expected to change immediately to a new agenda. The adults didn't get to ease into a new way of working by exploring what interested them — they were forced to do things the new way whether it appealed to them or not. They weren't being mentored thoughtfully — they were being ordered to do as they were told. Exactly the opposite of what the administrators wanted to champion for their students.

Surprisingly often, people will champion self-directed learning for children but not allow those children's parents the same freedom and respect. It's their way or the highway, and you had better start doing it the right way (their way) *right away*. Your kids should learn at their own pace, follow their interests, and you should trust that they'll eventually learn everything they need to know. You, on the other hand, should get with the program, right now, 100%, or else. You don't need to have your own opinions or ideas; ours will suffice. There's no time to experiment and see if these ideas work for you; take it on faith or you're part of the problem.

If your child deserves to learn at his own pace and have his own ideas, so do you. Whatever you champion for your child, make sure you also give to yourself: the right to follow your own path, work at your own pace, follow your own interests, make mistakes, and try again. Whatever you want for your children, you are far more likely to help them achieve it if you live it yourself.

I hope you find inspiration in these pages. Not the empty sort — pretty and two-dimensional — that stays separate from your real life, but something you can really put to use.

The freedom that we have to create a life that works for us, our children, and our families is priceless. We should never trade it for a handful of magic beans — a purist approach that comes with a set of pregummed labels, a rule book an inch thick, and threat of eviction from the tribe if you deviate from the center of the path. As you explore new ideas — in this book and elsewhere — about how children learn and how we can help them learn, I hope you keep a firm grip on your own opinions and values. You can build a life customized to your beliefs and priorities. Don't settle for off-the-rack.

The philosophy of project-based homeschooling — this particular approach to helping children become strong thinkers, learners, and doers — is dependent upon the interest and the enthusiastic participation and leadership of the learners themselves, the children. The ideas in this book are offered to you in the same spirit: follow your interests, build something new, and make it your own.

A Way to Learn

What is the point of learning? What is education for?

Many children have pondered those questions while sitting at a desk intensely bored, listening to a teacher drone on about something that neither interested them nor seemed useful.

> "Well, Mr. Snelgrove, I happen to know that in the future
> I will not have the slightest use for algebra, and I speak
> from experience." — *Peggy Sue Got Married*

How many children realize that education is for *them*, so they can do whatever they want to do in life — build a robot, design wedding dresses, write comic books, take care of animals at the zoo? How many relate what's in front of them — whether it's a history book, a math book, or a spelling test — to something they really care about?

If they did put it together — if they added 2 and 2 and came up with the answer that this is *their* education, meant to help them live whatever life they choose — they might stand up and demand that it be more interesting and more relevant. They might say, hey, if this boat is for me, then I want to sail over *there*.

Imagine if public-school teachers had to justify to their students that what they were studying was relevant and would be useful in the future. Could they do it? Could you?

When we set out as a society to educate children, we create a curriculum — *what* they will study — and a pedagogy — *how* we will teach it. By and large, in the public schools, over many decades, this can be boiled down to *What Every Fifth Grader Should Know* and rote.

Many interesting things are happening in private schools, magnet schools, charter schools, and various public schools, but they never seem to make the jump to standard practice. "Innovations" in education — child-led learning, long-term projects, hands-on experiences, and etc. — are not new ideas. John Dewey, Bank Street, Reggio Emilia, project-based learning — educators have been championing these methods for a very long time. They simply seem new because they never gain any traction, so when they are (continually) reintroduced, the fresh new audience isn't familiar with them. "Huzzah!," says the audience. "This is what we've been needing!" And they champion those same ideas once again. And once again, wondrous things happen here and there, but mostly everything stays the same.

> "Think of how vastly different our world of today is from even one hundred years ago. Someone traveling through time would hardly recognize the country, as we know it today. Yet, if that same time-traveler were to walk into today's classroom, it would be far more familiar. Instruction is teacher-directed, lecture-oriented and textbook driven and spelling tests are still given on Fridays. Drill and practice is the focus of reinforcing concepts. Basal readers pound the shelves and desks with linear comprehension skills and phonics." — Karen Morse, "When Schools Fail"

From *The Adventures of Tom Sawyer* to *Calvin and Hobbes*, it is historically acknowledged that children more or less do not enjoy the educational process as a rule.

> "Why'n earth they want us to go to school *any*way?" Stuart demanded.

> "Old first grade," Robert said.

> "Why," I said treacherously, "first thing you know you'll

be having a wonderful time in school. You've just forgotten what school is *like*."

"*No*, we haven't," Robert said.

"*I* used to *love* school," I said.

This was a falsehood so patent that none of them felt it necessary to answer me, even in courtesy. They sat and stared at me instead. — Shirley Jackson, *Life Among the Savages*

The standard public educational process has little to nothing to do with the individual child and what he or she enjoys/detests, is interested in/bored by, has talent for/a complete lack of talent for. The child is expected to bend to what society wants in terms of their education and their future occupation.

We set a plateful of cafeteria stew down in front of the child and order him to eat up. "Yes, I know the gravy is gray and lumpy, and the stew is liberally dotted with peas, which you despise, but eat up. It's good for you."

We create a curriculum — a list of knowledge and skills we deem important for all children to learn — and then we deliver that same curriculum to all of the children and expect them to clean their plates.

When we talk about project-based homeschooling, we are moving beyond knowledge and skills and probing underneath for the machinery of learning. We are thinking less about the specific facts that will be learned (radius of Mars, exports of Peru) and more about what makes a person want to learn and how we can help them become adept at doing the things they want to do.

Rather than filling our child's educational plate and saying, "Eat up. Trust me. This is what you need," we hand them the menu and say, "Order something that looks good to you."

(Keep in mind: Helping your child direct and manage his own learning does not mean immediately giving him complete control of his entire curriculum. You can balance assigned work with self-chosen work. We are talking about that essential portion of your child's learning life that you will devote to helping him do his own self-chosen work — you get to decide how big that portion will be.)

Project-based homeschooling isn't a wrestling match or a power struggle, because the child gets to learn about whatever interests him. Rather than educating him with a carrot or a stick, we are taking a half-step back and saying, "I'm here to help you in whatever way I can." We become mentors, sharing our thinking and learning skills and hopefully transferring them. We become stronger learners ourselves as we work with our child.

When you say to a child, "I get to pick what you're learning, and I get to pick how you learn it and how you prove to me that you know it," then we should really expect to get little back in the form of emotional investment. They may obey, and they may even respect our opinion and make a good effort (or they may not), but in no way should we expect that they will be really, truly excited about what they're learning, unless we've managed to magically hit upon just the thing that they happen to care deeply about.

And even if we do, woe to the child, because we have a complete

Self-chosen work is self-motivated.

curriculum to work our way through, and we'll be moving on after this brief unit. But they're free to continue to learn about it in their own free time, such as it is.

In project-based homeschooling, you zero in on what interests your child and stay there as long as she is interested. She's not on her own; you're there with materials, support, feedback, interest. With the same enthusiasm and passion that you might transfer a beloved skill (breadmaking, woodworking, tennis), you help your child acquire the skills to think, learn, make, and do.

The importance of a child's authentic interest cannot be over-emphasized. Without it, learning is like pushing a boulder uphill. With it, we're pushing the boulder downhill. Learning occurs in both directions. So why do we usually go with the uphill option? It boils down to fear. Or, nervousness. Nervousness that a child won't get all the important knowledge that he needs (radius of Mars, exports of Peru). Nervousness that a child who is allowed to pursue his own interests won't learn the important lessons of how to buckle down and do work that is boring, uninteresting, and meaningless. And so on.

Homeschooling parents have the same fears as society at large, but even more intense, because their concern is for their own child versus a faceless group of society's children. It's one thing to think of a generation of kids who might not know *What Every Fifth Grader*

Should Know. It's another to think fearfully of your own beloved child competing against a generation of kids who might have some key bit of information or crucial skill that your child does not.

Every parent who decides to take responsibility for their child's education must take this on. (Although, shhh — here's a secret — actually *all* parents are responsible for their child's education, even if they send them to school. Remember that in your darker moments.)

But think about this. Imagine, after fifteen years or so, you have two children who've managed to graduate with educational deficits. Which would you rather have: the child who has some holes in her knowledge and skills? Or the child whose thinking and learning machinery is rusty from disuse? An enthusiastic and creative learner who is missing a few facts? Or the child who memorized those facts but who says "I hate to read"?

The child who is a skilled thinker and adept learner can adjust to whatever the future doles out. She can spackle in those holes in her knowledge, and she knows how to acquire skills she needs to do things she wants to do. On the other hand, the child who shoveled down his prepared education but lost his curiosity, whose interests withered away and were replaced by a general malaise and desire to just be left alone — that child has a bagful of knowledge and skills with varying expiration dates and dubious ability or desire to acquire more.

After we graduate, we're in charge of our own learning. We may read or not read, we may learn or not learn — it's our choice. If we don't segue into adulthood with a solid acquaintance with the deep pleasures of learning and work, we may never meet them later in life.

Project-based homeschooling is concerned with the underlying motives, habits, and attitudes of thinking and learning. However you feel about knowledge and skills — whether you're a Latin-loving classicist or a relaxed unschooler or somewhere in-between — the point of project-based homeschooling is to devote *some* time to helping your child direct and manage his own learning. This does not have to comprise your entire curriculum. (Though it can.) It does not have to be the primary focus of your learning life. (Though it can be.) But it is essential. It is the part of your child's education that is focused on that underlying machinery. It is the part of your child's learning life that is focused on your child's very specific and unique interests, talents, and passions. It is the part of your child's learning when he is not only free to explore whatever interests him, but he receives attention, support, and consistent, dependable mentoring to help him succeed.

Allowing children to learn about what interests them is good, but helping them do it in a meaningful, rigorous way is better. Freedom and choice are good, but a life steeped in thinking, learning, and doing is better. It's not enough to say, "Go, do whatever you like." To help children become skilled thinkers and learners, to help them become people who make and do, we need a life centered around those experiences. We need to show them how to accomplish the things they want to do. We need to prepare them to make the life they want.

To be a mentor goes beyond showing a child how to use the library or bind a book, bake a muffin or build a birdhouse. It means setting an example of what it means to be an alert, curious, interested human being. It means setting an example of doing, making, creating, and sharing. "Lifelong learning" is a phrase so trite it makes your teeth hurt, but being a good mentor means showing your child that learning doesn't stop when someone hands you a diploma. Not by treacly speech, but by everyday immersion in a life that celebrates learning interesting things and doing challenging, meaningful work.

Project-based homeschooling is a way to learn. It doesn't have to be the only way you learn, but it is an absolutely essential experience for children — to spend time working on something that matters and to spend time working with a dedicated mentor.

It is a way to learn that sets aside the importance of subject matter and focuses on what it means to be an accomplished thinker, learner, maker, and doer. In pursuing her own meaningful work — her project work — your child may miss something that you believe is absolutely crucial to learn. If that happens (and if it's important to you), you can simply make sure she learns it separately, in whatever way you think is best. But project work is the time when your child is in charge of determining *what* is learned and *how* she will learn it.

The only person she will have to satisfy about whether she learned it well enough is herself. She'll set her own goals and figure out how to meet them, with your help.

Self-Directed, Self-Managed

What does project-based homeschooling look like?

I've worked with my own homeschooled children, other people's homeschooled children in small and large groups, and the children who attended my private school. For several years I ran an after-school program attended by public-schooled children. I've had the privilege of working with kids ranging in age from 2 to 15 who had experienced a wide range of learning environments.

All of these children created amazing projects. It didn't matter whether they were home- or public- or private-schooled; it didn't matter whether they worked alone or with a friend or in a large group. What defined their work was ownership. They directed and managed the project. They owned the work. And the work they created was amazing.

Real project work is work that is chosen by children and done by children, with the help of attentive adults who are there to mentor, facilitate, and support.

I have visited schools that purported to have a project-based curriculum, but the teachers told the kids what to do. The kids were bored and uninvested in what was happening in their "project." They were given some small, meaningless choices: "Do you want to be in this group or that group?" "Do you want to do this activity or that

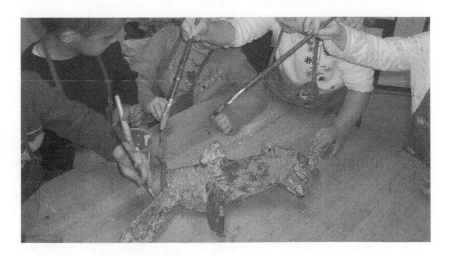

The children must own the work.

activity?" But they weren't having any meaningful effect on what was going on in their classroom. They weren't directing or managing the project or their own learning. And they knew it. I'm not sure whether the teachers knew it.

In contrast, I have visited schools that purported to have a completely traditional curriculum, but the teacher (a wizard) was expert at letting the children lead. The kids were having big ideas, they were figuring out how to make those ideas happen, and the teacher was there to help them. It was a negotiated curriculum: the teacher expected hard work and collaboration, and the students expected autonomy and influence. The children owned the work, and they knew it.

It doesn't matter what label you stick on it; what matters is what is really happening in the room. Are the kids working independently? Are they making the plans and figuring out how to turn those plans into reality? Are they making mistakes, arguing with one another, and deciding what to do next? Are they dividing up the jobs, offering each other help, and breaking up into natural small groups to attack various tasks? Are they confidently going up to their teacher or parent to make a request for materials or assistance?

Are the adults in the room paying attention to what's happening? Are they taking notes and photographs? Are they guiding the children to work through disagreements and settle arguments? Have they created a system so plans aren't forgotten? Have they made a workspace that allows the children to work independently? Does that workspace obviously honor the work being done there?

The authenticity of the work is what's important. The ownership of the ideas, the control over decision-making. The roles are important: the children must direct their own learning, and the adults must steadfastly support that.

What does project-based learning look like?

> A group of children age three to five are working together to build a large, three-dimensional cardboard whale. Two are crouched on the floor looking at a book, shouting out information and ideas to the others. Two are arguing about fin design — they decide they will each make one fin the way they prefer and they'll use both. Another decides to make krill for the whale to eat, so he sits down and begins cutting paper into tiny pieces. An adult sits with them, making careful notes about their plans: what they need (more cardboard, tape, paint), what they plan to do (build the fins, the teeth, the tail), what they disagree on (whether their whale should lie on the floor or hang from the ceiling). Later, she can use her notes to help the children remember all of their plans. One of the children walks up to her and asks her to write down the colors of paint they will need: he lists them. Another says he wants to measure how big the whale is — he would like it to be life-size. They begin to discuss the best way to measure, and one of the children runs to get a book from the bookshelf — he remembers which book mentioned the exact length of their whale, even though he can't read yet.

In a large group, a lot of things can be happening at once. Children will break into smaller groups or work alone to tackle a particular task. Can you see how much learning is happening here — and how much potential there is for more learning? Can the children make a life-size whale? The adult isn't telling them, "You can't do that. It would be huge. We don't have room." The adult is going to wait and let them go through the lengthy process of figuring it out on their own. Think of all the learning there: How will we measure? We must discuss it, argue about it, decide what to do. What kind of whale will we measure? Where do we find the information? Our whale is bigger than this room! Now what should we do? They get to experience every bit of the learning, step by step. There's no rush. This is what projects are for.

> A ten-year-old boy is working on a comic project. He's started an online comic club, and he goes through the new entries on the shared blog he's set up, then e-mails one of the members about this week's drawing challenge. He is working on a letter to a famous cartoonist, and he is carefully decorating the envelope with the cartoonist's characters. He stops and pulls over a pad of sticky notes and makes a note about something he wants to look up at the library; he sticks it on the wall above his table and goes back to work.

Here is a child deeply engaged in his meaningful work. He's reading about comics and making his own comics. He's corresponding with artists. He's working at home, alone, but he's in contact with other children with similar interests doing similar work. Notice how, even at home, alone, he's making important connections with other people through letters, through the computer. Tomorrow he might be working at a table with two friends, making a comic book, but even when he's working alone, he is part of a larger community.

> A small group of three- to five-year-olds are playing library. They've arranged a small table and a book-shelf and they are taking turns playing librarian and customers. The librarian stamps the inside of the books with a small block. One child says, "We need book-marks. The librarian always gives me a bookmark." An adult sits nearby listening and making notes in a journal, taking an occasional photograph. The children are used

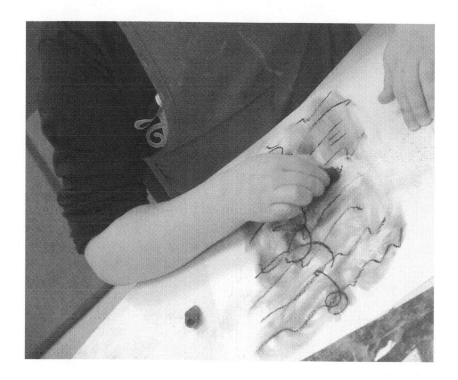

to this and pay no attention. One of them crouches down and waves a hand under the table. "This part should not be see-through." Another child agrees: "That's where we put the books we bring back."

Children learn through play. This is more obvious with small children: they play-act, they take on adult roles, they explore how the world works. Their play churns up questions, ideas, disagreements — all rich material for project learning. An attentive adult can help them remember their questions and plans. Later, when they are gathered around making art, the adult will say, "Haley wanted to make the bottom of the table solid, and Mark said you need a book return — does anyone want to work on that? We've hung up the pictures we took at the library and the sketches you made."

Older children also learn through play. They take photographs, keep sketchbooks, write stories. They make stop-motion films, act out skits, write songs, draw comics. They're also working out how the world works — and they're starting to make their own contributions.

> A six-year-old boy is working at an easel, doing a large painting of a bird. He refers often to a small pencil sketch he drew the previous week. Spread on the table next to him are some reference books. Later, he'll take a photo of his work-in-progress and upload it to his blog. On the other side of the easel is his younger sister. She is also painting a bird. Her brother's interest in birds has, in turn, made her interested. She asks him how to draw a wing. He comes around the easel and looks at her work critically. He brings her to the table and shows her photos of birds in his library books. He asks his father if he will read the part about wings aloud to them while they paint.

Children thrive in mixed-age groups, whether they are working with siblings or neighborhood friends or classmates. In a large group, the excitement and passion of one or two children can infect the whole group — everyone wants to learn about pirate ships or seashells or castles because those children share their excitement. Younger siblings and younger group members will get involved at the level appropriate for them if you let them. Very young children can ask astute questions and make meaningful contributions.

Eventually, the younger children in the group will be older and they'll be driving the project. Ideally, all children should be given the opportunity to be both the mentor and the mentee, the oldest and the youngest, the one who gives and the one who receives help. In a school or co-op, this can happen with multiage classrooms and/or teachers/facilitators who stay with students for more than one year. At home, we need to make sure our children have the opportunity to work with both younger and older children.

> Several children are working in a project group learning about frogs. Today, they are doing clay sculptures. An aquarium sits in the center of the table, holding three different varieties of tree frog. The children are talking

as they work, asking questions, arguing, informing one another about what they know about these frogs. One adult is taking notes — keeping track of those questions and disagreements for later discussion. Another is showing two children how to make slip so they can attach legs to their frog bodies. One child decides to roll her clay flat and carve a scene about frogs instead of making her frog three-dimensional. A few other children follow her example and roll their clay flat as well.

Children working together inspire one another. A child has an idea and creates something; his friend sees what he has made and wants to do it, too. He copies the first child's creation, but he does something extra — he adds something new. He extends the idea. He adds some detail that the first child overlooked or solves a problem in a unique and better way. The first child sees what his friend has done and goes back to add it to his own creation. They are extending and building upon one another's ideas.

Look for opportunities for your child to work with other children. It doesn't have to be a formal project group; you can simply invite friends over to draw, paint, or build models with you. The other children don't have to join in for the entire project; their questions, ideas, and collaboration will still add a tremendous amount to the work your child is doing.

Sharing and exchanging ideas.

Even in a group, each child brings his own ideas and follows his own interests.

These are just a few projects. Each project is unique because all of the elements are unique — different children have different specific interests and they express themselves in different ways. They home in on what interests them particularly, and what they choose to do with their knowledge — what they build — is always unique. In a group setting, individual children will each focus on the particular aspect that interests them the most. They'll tell each other about what they learn, they'll copy each other's ideas and representations, and eventually they'll all share the same knowledge. But each has made a unique contribution to the whole; each has had a slightly different learning experience because each chose his own path.

The crucial thing to notice about each of these different scenarios is that the children are excited, engaged, and pursuing work that's important to them. The adults are there to support, but the children are driving the process.

Identifying Interests

Whether you are working with one child or a group, the first step is to find out what your child wants to know more about. This is where the work starts. You can find this starting point in one of two ways: you can ask or you can observe.

If you ask your child what he wants to study, a very small child may not really grasp what you mean. He may shout out a lot of different ideas — candy corn! snakes! cowboys! — none of which, you suspect, are an authentic deep interest. You might be better off observing his play and his conversation. What does he ask about? What does he build with blocks? What does he play-act? What does he beg to watch on TV or film? Which books does he ask for again and again? If you make careful notes over several days, you may find an area in which your child already has a strong interest. You can then begin to feed that interest.

Older children who are experienced with project work will simply tell you what they want to do next. I want to learn about *this*: corn snakes, space shuttles, doll-making, beetles. They already know how projects work. They have ideas about where they want to go and what they want to make. They expect to direct and manage their learning. They own the process.

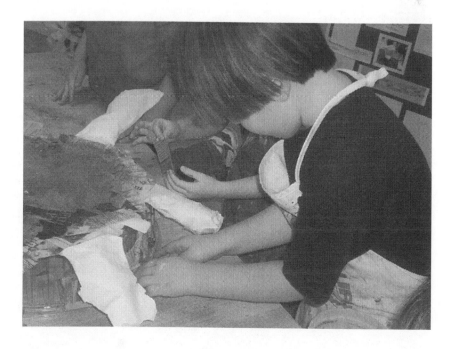

Older children who are new to project work may be suspicious about your motives. Most children are familiar with how fast adults can suck the fun out of any subject by making it educational. They may strongly prefer that you stay far, far away from their favorite subjects. This is another time when it might be more useful to simply observe and then feed the interest that already exists.

When you do this, however, be aware that your child still may not trust your motives. Why are you suddenly so interested, Mom and Dad? Are you going to ruin this for me? Are you going to turn my favorite thing into homework?

You know your child best. You can sit down and talk with them plainly and say, "We want you to have time to learn about what matters most to you, what interests you most. And we want to give you what you need to do that. I want to talk to you about it and help you." Or you can be stealthy and simply start offering up the time, space, materials, and attention that your child needs to take his learning to a deeper level.

The Earlier, the Better

Every suggestion in this book is easier if you are working with a young child — preferably between the ages of two and four. It's certainly not impossible with an older child; there is no age at which it's too late to introduce these ideas. You are older, after all, than your children, and it's not too late for you. On the other hand, your child — whether she's been educated in school or at home — already has definite ideas about learning, working, and how things are supposed to happen. If you establish a strong family culture and a daily routine that celebrates meaningful work when your child is very young, she will grow up with one set of expectations. If this is all new and different, you'll have to deal with a different set.

Take it slow and give your children (and yourself) time to adjust. The whole point is to give them the opportunity to be in charge of their own learning; therefore, it makes no sense to force it on them or try to rush the process.

But if you have the opportunity, start early.

Preparing the Environment

In the famous preschools of Reggio Emilia, each class has two co-teachers. The environment (the classroom, school, and play-ground/garden) is referred to as "the third teacher" because of the impact it has on the students: the messages it sends, what it allows, what it encourages, what it says to and about the children.

If you want your child to be in control of his own work, your environment can either help or hinder that goal. Can your child reach the materials he needs, or does he have to ask you to get things down for him? Can he put away his own things when he's through? Can he clean up his own mess, or do you have to do it?

You may say the words, "I want my child to be independent," but if your environment strongly sends the opposite message, you are working at cross-purposes.

Ideally, you want the environment to support all of your goals and values. As you figure out what your goals are, take a hard look at your surroundings: arc they helping you or hurting you?

Your child needs a dedicated workspace — a desk or table along with some nearby wall space and somewhere to keep materials. This space should be located somewhere that your child actually wants to be. If you stick his desk in his bedroom but you spend all your time in the kitchen, what will happen? It usually works best if his workspace is near the heart of your home: the place where everyone tends to be during the day.

A dedicated workspace serves several functions:

It reminds your child of what he's working on and why. He sees his work every day, and he's reminded of his interests and his plans. A bulletin board on the wall gives him a place to hang up sketches, notes, posters, and lists of questions to be answered. His unfinished projects on display and his sketches on his bulletin board remind him of his exciting plans. His space can be his science lab, his workshop, his art studio — it's full of interesting materials and projects just waiting for him to begin. It surrounds him with visual reminders of what he was working on yesterday and what he wanted to do today. His workspace tells the story of his project — and it tells a story about your child as a learner.

Your child's workspace reminds him daily of his plans and intentions. His books, his sketches, his photos, his unfinished artwork and models — make sure they're on display, so they can remind and inspire him daily.

It helps your child stay in the flow. Project work is partly about the topic and partly about meta-learning: learning about learning. An engaged child is busy creating new knowledge: thinking, having ideas, making plans, solving problems. When someone else has to help him find some paper, get paintbrushes down from a high cabinet, or hover over him to make sure he doesn't spill paint, he not only loses focus, he loses the opportunity to practice being independent and responsible.

If your child needs to go in search of a tool (scissors, tape, paper), he's that much more likely to abandon his idea or become fatally distracted. Having the necessary tools, materials, and resources at his fingertips allows him to focus on his ideas and concentrate on constructing knowledge.

It sends a message that your child is capable. A workspace organized for independence sends a message that your child is strong and capable. Your child is free to direct and manage her own work. She knows where everything goes — there's a place for her books, her pencils, her paper, her magnifying glass, her scissors, her tape. She can get what she needs without asking for help, and she can put things away again on her own. She can be independent and responsible, which is what she wants.

She can help you figure out the most useful way to sort and organize her tools and materials, and she should be able to do the work of tidying her space on her own. She is in charge of the space, and she is in charge of the learning that happens there.

It sends a message that you value your child's work. By honoring your child's work with an appropriate space and quality materials, you make a strong statement about its value to your family. Look at how your child's space is arranged. Look at her materials. See how her work is displayed. Be sure that the environment is sending a clear message: *Your work is important.*

You are creating an environment that supports the type of work you want your child to be able to do.

He chooses his own work, based on what interests and engages him. You encourage the values of deep investigation, expression, exploration, thinking, learning, sharing.

Create an environment that has what he needs so he can concentrate on his ideas.

Think about your space. Does it attract? Does it inspire? Does it tell the story of your child's work and interests? Is it the workspace of an active, independent, creative person? Is it the space of an explorer, an investigator, an artist, a scientist? Does it encourage creation and invention? Does it allow independence and joyful making?

The space you create plays a key role in creating the experiences your child will have. You can change the kind of work your child does by changing his environment. You can encourage him to work larger by clearing out a larger space. You can allow him to take on more responsibility by putting his materials where he can reach them and manage them on his own. You can help him realize he's capable by giving him the supplies and opportunity to clean up his own mess.

Every choice you make in his environment should reflect your values for how you want him to work, think, and learn.

Schedule/Routine

In order to do meaningful, personal work, your child needs time to think, explore, and play. In order to do the deep work of long-term

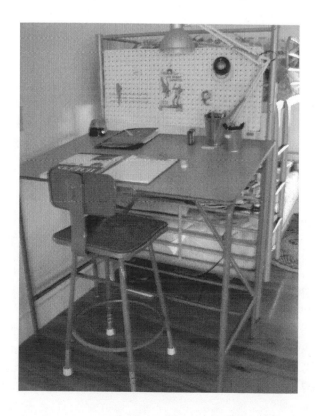

project learning, your child needs to come back to his work regularly. It needs to become something he anticipates and depends on.

If you follow a more traditional curriculum, you'll need to set aside special time reserved for project work. Remember that project learning requires exploring, thinking, playing, talking, and planning, not only creating books, constructions, and works of art. Project time is focused but flexible; project work is serious but playful. Relax and concentrate on seeing how your child uses this time and what results. Observe, journal, and reflect.

If you're a more eclectic homeschooler, project learning could be the main focus of your curriculum, possibly meeting most of your learning goals. You still need to respect the ebb and flow of natural learning. Your child can't be "on" 100% of the time, always making, always building, always creating. You must allow for what Barbara Ueland calls the "dreamy time" that comes before creative work, when your child is "letting in ideas." There must always be time to explore and play.

Try to avoid pulling attention away from your child's project (his deepest interest) with random, one-off activities. Save casual field trips and similar activities for times between projects. The less you distract your child with random activities and interruptions, the more engaged and focused he'll be. You're giving him the opportunity to stay longer with what he cares about most; you're giving him the chance to build something really meaningful.

Whenever possible, field trips and events should be integrated with his project. Rather than setting up an unrelated craft, provide open-ended art experiences that your child can use to explore project-related ideas. Rather than attending a random event, let him plan a project-related field trip and invite friends along.

Look critically at your family's week and consider whether your child's scheduled activities leave enough time for relaxed play, reading, open-ended making and creating, and unhurried exploration. Do you have enough big blocks of relaxed, unscheduled time? Does your child have enough free time to do all the things he wants to do? Do you have enough dedicated project time to keep his interest alive and let his work build momentum?

Children need big blocks of unscheduled time.

In your daily schedule, avoid numerous and/or unnecessary transitions. If possible, plan for free time to follow project time, so your child can stay with his work longer if he chooses. You're striving to make it possible for him to become deeply engaged in his work; the last thing you want is to have to interrupt him to go do something else.

If you unschool, you probably have plenty of free time for exploration, but remember to make a deliberate and purposeful effort to support your child to dig deeply into her interests and challenge herself to extend her ideas. Even if your child is free to follow her interests 100% of the time, you can still set aside time when you will work with her and focus on helping her make her ideas happen. Dedicated time and support can allow your child to do deeper and more challenging work. Unschooling offers the time, flexibility, and freedom for children to really tap into their interests and talents and become passionate, relentless learners. Your attention and conscious support can encourage your child to stay with those interests longer and explore her passions in a way that simultaneously develops critical thinking and learning skills. Your focus helps her focus — on what matters to her most.

If you set aside blocks of time for project work, your child will know that he has your undivided attention during that time, that you'll be available to work with him (e.g., to read aloud to a pre-reader or write down his dictated book, to take an older child to the library or to do fieldwork, to help with special art activities, to organize a group work session, or just to brainstorm and offer feedback). He'll know that materials he's requested will be ready then. He'll know you'll be available to talk, listen, bounce ideas around, or just hang out together. He'll begin to count on this time — and anticipate it.

Project work obviously doesn't have to be done only during these periods of time. Your child can work on his project whenever he likes. But these dedicated times show him how much you value his work. He'll know that during these special blocks of time, you'll be

giving him and his work your attention and focus. He'll know this time is sacred and he can count on it. He can relax and know you'll keep coming back to the work and bringing him what he needs. With you as a mentor and collaborator, he can dig deeper, go further, do more.

You may be thinking, "Hey, I always support his interests and if he's truly interested, he'll pursue the work on his own." But setting aside time for project work becomes a self-fulfilling prophecy — it attracts the work you value. You are communicating (without words), "This work is so important to us that we dedicate time and attention to it." You are sending the message that "This is what we care about — this is what we're willing to work for."

Devoting that time allows you and your child to come together and fill it with something meaningful. You don't have to think about it, remember it, or squeeze it in — because it's so valued, it's a regular part of your routine.

If project work is left to simply happen when it happens, it may not happen at all. Your focus and attention create a gentle gravity that pulls your child back to his work. And remember: *it's work he wants to do*. Setting aside time for project work is a way of honoring it and making sure it happens.

If you do set aside scheduled time for working on projects, children should never be forced to work on their project during that time. It should simply be an option; it should be a time when you're available and able to give your child your full attention, when materials are ready, when plans are recalled and possibilities are discussed. Coercing or forcing a child to do project work removes the most important criteria — that it is self-chosen. During project time, a child might work on something else, read, create art, play, or simply think. Over time, however, scheduled project time tends to draw children to their work ... because you are ready, available, interested, focused ... because his space and his materials are ready ... because he has built a habit of returning regularly to his work ... because he is reminded of his plans and his excitement ... because he enjoys it.

Setting aside special time for working on projects communicates that this work is valued, respected, and celebrated by your family.

Your time, your attention, his workspace and materials, your observing and documenting, his ongoing work on display — these things send a strong message that this is something very meaningful and important to your family, something you care about deeply.

When you schedule the time, you make a commitment — to him, to yourself, to the work. When you make a commitment, you show your child what you value. When you follow through, you teach him to count on it, depend on it, and bring his best efforts.

Tools and Materials

The more varied your child's choices in available materials, the more complex his representations will be.

What are "representations"? They are the manifestations of his learning: what he creates. What form do those representations take? They take an immense variety of forms: drawing, painting, collage, sculpture, modeling, storytelling, book-making, film-making, theatre, dramatic play...

Much of what he creates will be in the form of two- and three-

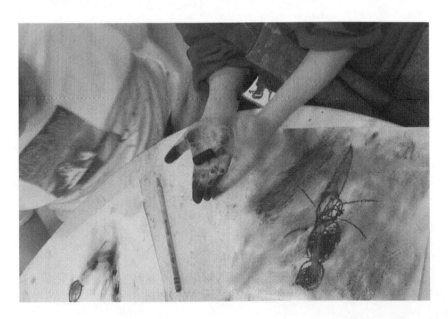

dimensional artworks. Even dramatic play is enhanced with costumes and props he makes himself. Story-, song-, and book-writing are enhanced by the materials at hand for capturing them and presenting them to others: writing materials, paper, typewriter, computer, book-binding supplies, musical instruments, cameras, videocameras. The work your child produces will be shaped by the quality, variety, and accessibility of his tools and materials.

Better-quality art supplies make for more beautiful representations and encourage your child to put more care into their making. Nothing is more attractive and tempting than a gorgeous array of colored pencils and paints attractively displayed with lovely paper of different sizes and finishes. Higher-quality art materials have more vibrant colors than their cheaper counterparts. They also last longer, so choosing better materials may not cost much more in the long run.

High-quality materials arranged beautifully send a message to your child that his work is important and valued. They say, "I can't wait to see what you do with these." They say, "Your work matters. You deserve the best."

Higher-quality colored pencils, oil pastels, and watercolor paints have clearer, brighter colors. Better paper has a better feel and shows brighter colors. Your child will be irresistibly attracted to using beautiful materials, and those materials have a better chance of representing his ideas as beautifully as he imagined them. Quality materials inspire quality work.

If your child is tremendously prolific, there's nothing wrong with discussing the relative expense of various materials and encouraging him to use cheaper materials for sketches and first drafts and save the best materials for final drafts and/or the work that matters most. Weighing his own work's relative importance and deciding whether it deserves the best materials is a skill that he can master. Learning to begin with a rough sketch and proceed through multiple drafts to a finished piece is a process that helps every maker, whether they are an artist, chef, engineer, or architect.

If your child is very young, you can help him by making sure he has everyday access to good-quality, reasonably priced materials (e.g, copy paper) and bringing out the best materials (e.g., heavier paper or a stretched canvas) when he's working on later versions of important representations.

The process of introducing a new workspace, new materials, and a new routine can be exciting and challenging at the same time.

Go slow. Keep your expectations reasonable. You won't set up your workspace on Monday, fill it with new materials, and be doing awesome project work by Wednesday. Give yourself and your child time to get used to a new routine, explore new materials, and think about interesting things she might like to do. There's no rush.

Introduce new tools and materials slowly, one at a time. Aim for eventual abundance, but take your time getting there. Start with the basics — good paper, drawing and painting supplies, clean recyclables and tape for building. Whenever you add something new, take time for a lengthy period of relaxed exploration.

Talk about each new material. This is especially helpful if you're working with more than one child. Discuss: What can we do with this? What should we *not* do with it? How do we clean it up and put

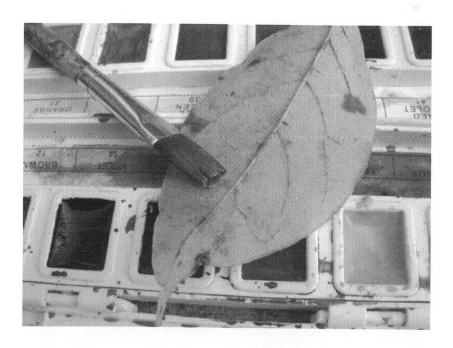

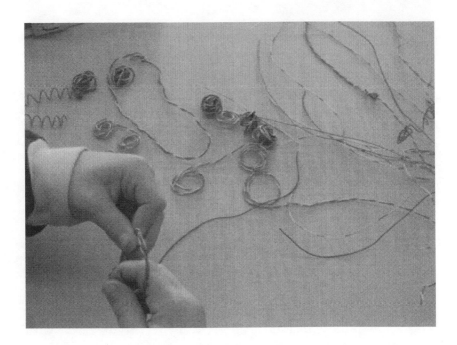

it away again? This applies to everything from paint to blocks. If you introduce things slowly, over a period of days or weeks, your child can spend time excited about each material, exploring it thoroughly. She'll give each addition her entire focus, because it's new and interesting. She won't be distracted by a studio or workspace chockablock with shiny new materials.

The relaxed introduction of materials translates into a relaxed pace when learning and making. Concentrate on the quality of experience that you want your child to have: free exploration before purposeful work, thoughtful planning before execution.

Exploring each material freely for a time allows your child to get to know what it can do and how it works, its possibilities and its limitations. You can guide discussion about the materials and their properties. Talk about what happens when you paint two colors next to each other and both are wet. What about when one is wet and one is dry? Compare different effects produced while messing around. Later, your child can repeat these effects deliberately when she chooses.

Free exploration gives your child the knowledge she needs to work purposefully when she's ready. Rather than becoming frustrated when her paints run together, she'll already know how to manipulate the paint to do what she wants. By learning about a material when she's relaxed and simply playing and exploring, she'll be fluent in that medium when she's ready to create something specific. She'll reach for tools and materials with confidence.

By starting with relaxed exploration, you've separated the process of learning about the material from using it for a purpose to meet a specific goal. This is an important part of project-based homeschooling: breaking down the learning process and getting to understand how it works. Before we create something important, there are a lot of smaller steps we have to take. This is how we master a skill, a tool, a material, a technique — through play, through practice, through making and fixing mistakes.

This time of introducing various art-making materials and freely exploring them while talking and enjoying each other's company is a great time to listen and look for clues to possible interests for project work. What does your child draw and paint and sculpt for fun?

If you have more than one child doing project work together, they may need to learn to trust the abundance of materials in the art studio or workspace. They may want to glue thirty buttons to a single piece of paper — they would rather use up all the materials than risk having them used up by someone else. Rather than setting limiting rules like "three buttons per person per day," you might want to ride it out and let them see that when they use things up, they'll be replaced. (It can help to start by offering cheaper materials first. Popsicle sticks come to mind.) Let them learn that they can trust the abundance — that materials will be replaced as they're used. They can relax and stop worrying about buttons and concentrate on their work.

Follow a pattern of bringing in new materials and tools one at a time, discussing their possibilities, then encouraging lots of free exploration. Let your child try out his new cleaning materials and responsibilities. Help him decide how to organize the space, and encourage him to make suggestions for improvements or additions.

If these are big changes, it makes sense to introduce them slowly and get used to a new way of doing things before you add the pressure of starting a project.

Introduce project tools into your regular day. Take clipboards and pencils along when you run errands and encourage your children to sketch interesting things they see. Take watercolors on your walk at the park. Talk at dinner about the work you did that day (painting a picture, examining worms in the garden). Make blank books from folded and stapled paper and have your pre-reader dictate stories for you to write, then encourage them to do the illustrations.

You are beginning to build new habits — a way of looking at and talking about your day. You are introducing the elements of project-based homeschooling before applying them to a specific topic.

Introduce routines the same way. Set aside dedicated project time even before you start a project. Use this time to explore new art, construction, or play materials. Use it to get used to your new workspace. Before you work, talk about your plans. Afterward, talk about what you did. Share it with the whole family at dinner. Ease into your new way of learning.

You need space and time to tinker, play, explore, and experiment. It's no use having the space if you don't have the time. It's no use having the time if you don't have the space. It's no use having materials if you don't have time to work with them or space to do it in.

This is what it means to commit to creating a supportive environment. You admit that all of the ingredients are necessary — space, materials, time. They're interdependent. You admit that without focus and attention, the magic moments are probably not going to happen, or there won't be nearly as many of them.

Make the space. Make the time. Gather the materials. Prioritize the experience. Commit.

This way, it can happen. You've set the stage for the kind of thinking and exploring and learning you want to nurture. You are making it possible for your child to do the purposeful work you want to encourage.

The Power of Your Attention

There are many things you can do to help your child direct and manage her own learning, but perhaps the most important one is choosing how and where to put your attention.

Think hard about what you value most, because that's what deserves your attention. Your child will respond by doing more of whatever earns your focus. You feed a behavior with your attention, and by feeding it, you create more of it — so be thoughtful about what you invest with that power. Contemplate your goals and intentions.

As your child's first collaborator, you're the first person who reacts, the first who asks a question, the first who notices a detail. Your attention shines a light on her work and shows it back to her. It helps her focus on what she cares about.

By paying attention to your child — really focusing on quietly observing her play, her conversation, her ideas, and her creations — you begin to highlight her interests, ideas, questions, desires, fears, and confusions. You begin to gather the data that helps you figure out how she learns and how you can help her learn.

By paying attention to her environment, you'll begin to see how each choice you make — about her materials and tools, their accessibility, how they're brought out and how they're put away, their quality, their size, their number — affects how your child plays, experiments, invents, works, and creates. Your purposeful attention begins to shape your child's learning.

Without being told, she notices what gets your attention. She sees that you care enough about her work to write about it in your journal, to photograph it, to talk with her about it seriously. Where you focus your attention sends a clear message about what you value.

You don't have to force your child to work. If you pull out your journal and camera and document her work, you communicate the importance of what she's doing. She'll respond to this clear message — she'll do more of it.

You ask what she needs and help her make a list. You help her write down her questions and hang them on the wall. You share her work with family and friends and display it prominently in your home. You make trips into the community to do fieldwork. You set aside time to read aloud the research materials she's chosen and help her locate information on the computer. You dedicate time, space, and attention to her interests and her investigations. You are creating a family culture that celebrates meaningful work.

You make a physical space for her to work. You gather her materials together in one dedicated spot. You highlight her sketches and plans. You help her label her drawings. You write her plans in your journal. You are honoring her work, and in turn, she honors it.

Your attention creates a dynamic that attracts your child and shows her the value of her own work. She responds by doing more of what you pay attention to — your attention to what matters becomes a self-fulfilling prophecy, creating more of what matters. By defining and prioritizing what you value, you create a way of living that automatically nurtures and encourages it.

Attention works on every level of this approach. When you make your child's workspace a priority — helping him create a clean, organized, attractive place to draw, write, build — and when you give him beautiful materials to work with, you make a place that draws him in and encourages his creativity without having to say a word. When you honor his work with your attention — taking photographs and notes, listening, responding — he is drawn to doing more of what earns that attention. By focusing on what he cares about most, you help him spend more time on what's important to *him*.

When your home, your routine, and your commitment are focused on your child's work, he won't need to hear you say you think it's important — he'll know it is.

Rather than using praise or coercion, you are simply choosing where to put your focus, what to feed with your attention. Therefore, you must be careful and deliberate about how you use this power. Remember the goals of project-based homeschooling: to help your child direct and manage his own learning, to help him make his ideas happen. Put your focus there.

Family Culture

Your family culture is the foundation of your child's learning life. It's the combination of your values and your habits. It is defined by what you care about and how you live — but mostly how you live.

Family culture is the hidden armature that gives structure to your daily life, including how you live and how you learn. What you believe, deep down, shows through. Family culture is the manifestation of your priorities — not what you say, not what you wish were true, but what you actually do on a daily basis. You create your family culture with your choices.

It determines everything about how you work, how you interact with each other and the world, and how you confront everything from problems to questions to interests to joy.

You can't separate how you approach life as a family and how your child will approach life as a thinker and learner. Your home is your child's first workplace, first studio, first school — and your family members are your child's first friends, first coworkers, first

audience, first collaborators. You are his first mentor, and his siblings are his first teammates. You can't separate learning from living. If your daily habits and routines don't support your learning goals, you need to get them back into alignment.

You want to build a family culture that celebrates and supports meaningful work. This is much more than *saying* the right thing — this is creating a lifestyle, a set of articulated beliefs, and a daily routine that encourage and sustain the life you want for your family.

Building a family culture means being purposeful with your choices. What you say you value pales in importance next to the way you live from day to day, the choices you make, big and small.

Consider the unspoken messages you send about your family's priorities and values. How do you spend most of your time together? Where do you spend it? If someone came into your home right now and walked around, looking at your walls and tables and shelves, seeing what's on display, what would they see? Do your surroundings reflect your priorities? Does your home tell the story of your family and what you value?

Now think about what messages your home, your routine, and your choices send to your child.

If your physical space says "explore, ask, make, share, create," but your underlying beliefs whisper "follow, obey, please me, don't make a mess," which message wins? Which will your child prioritize? Does one cancel the other out?

If you say to your child, "You are capable," but your space requires him to come to you for help setting up materials, cleaning up, finding tools, etc., then the environment is contradicting your words. It's sending a message of weakness, dependency, and inadequacy.

It's not just your physical environment that can help or hinder your goals. Think about the unspoken messages that your schedule, habits, daily rituals, and rules send. These messages will be heard loud and clear by your child. If they conflict with your words, your words will fade away.

Building a strong family culture that supports self-directed learning means aligning what you say with what you do and how you live. Be sure that your choices support your beliefs and your values.

Putting the Pieces Together

If you have

an honored space dedicated to doing meaningful work

and that space is full of

an interesting variety of high-quality materials and tools

and your routine offers

big chunks of time dedicated to spending time there,

then whatever your child does with those resources is worthwhile.

But...

add a strong, genuine interest

and you truly have something magical. Your child is bringing his highest attention and motivation to mix with the best learning environment you can offer.

Just messing around in a space like this is time well spent, but using the space, the materials, the tools, and the time to focus on something really interesting — something your child really cares about, fascinating questions and problems, big ideas — to build something real and significant... That is the ultimate goal of project-based homeschooling.

Doing the Work

Project-based homeschooling is an approach to learning that prioritizes doing real, meaningful work. That work must meet certain criteria.

It must be self-chosen. It must grow out of your child's genuine interest. His unique viewpoint and curiosity determine the path his project takes. He controls where the project goes.

It must be self-directed. If you are doing the planning and making the choices, what you have is a unit, not a project. Even if you choose a subject that you are absolutely sure your child will love, and even if he enjoys it, *if you do the planning, it is not a project.* The point of project-based homeschooling is not the topic — the objective is to give your child the chance to direct and manage his own learning. He decides what to do and how to do it.

It must be self-managed. Your child must set her own goals and measure her own progress. She must identify and then solve her own problems. You have to stay out of her way so she can do that. This can be very challenging for adults, especially if they feel it's their job to "teach" their child. They want to goose things along; they want to herd the child in the "right" direction. They want to point out what isn't going to work so time isn't wasted. But here's the thing — *it is not a waste of time for children to solve their own problems.* And to learn to solve problems requires being allowed to have them in the first place. Let them make mistakes.

Children need thoughtful support to do real, meaningful work.

> A group of children have been working together to make a car big enough for them to sit in. It is the size of a dining table and is made of an acre of cardboard and several thousand miles of tape.
>
> They've spent quite a bit of time looking at real cars. They've crawled inside and examined the pedals, the glove compartment, and the way the seatbelts work. They've made pencil sketches on clipboards, and their adult mentor has taken dozens of photographs to display above their work table along with their sketches.
>
> The last time they got together, they had a long discussion/argument about how to build the steering wheel. One child suggested pipe cleaners; the others said they were too small and flimsy. Another suggested cardboard tubes. They liked the tubular shape but were stymied by how they might be shaped into a circle.
>
> Today, a well-meaning parent comes into the room and announces, "I have a steering wheel for you!" She beams and holds up an actual steering wheel, found in a garage somewhere. She is full of cheer. One of the children runs forward to grab it. The two children who were working hard to solve the cardboard-tube problem are silent and deflated. Whatever learning was happening is over now; the adult has provided a solution.

Practice a wait-and-see attitude. Remember that even though things may seem to be moving interminably slowly to you, they are moving at the children's pace. Pay attention to what's really happening, take notes, take photographs — you may learn to see the change, the progress, the acquisition of skills and habits.

Mistakes and problems are opportunities to learn — not just facts like "School glue won't stick a heavy metal ball to a cardboard door" but deeper lessons like how to deal with frustration, how to articulate your opinion to the group, how to decide whose idea is best, how to overcome and forge ahead.

Project-based homeschooling isn't just about learning how to learn — it's about learning how to *think* and learning how to *do*. To learn how to think, we need to have a lot of rich experiences that stretch our minds in new directions. This doesn't mean collecting up a lot of random, unconnected events: zoo, aquarium, museum, airfield, animal hospital. Project-based homeschooling is about collecting up a lot of *related* experiences that work together to build real understanding. Your child makes the connections and provides the meaning. His project provides the context.

To learn how to think, we need to set some ambitious goals and

then hack our way toward them — no short-cuts. We need to use all of our abilities and skills. We need to work at the forward edge of our comfort zone. We need to confront the new, the confusing, and the contradictory.

To learn how to do, we need something real to focus on — not a task assigned by someone else, but something we want to create, something we want to understand. Not an empty exercise but a meaningful, self-chosen undertaking.

It's the difference between pretending to be a scientist and actually being a scientist. It's the difference between making a poster because someone required you to make one and making a poster because you really need a poster. It's a tiny but key change: the work is real. Everything is permeated with meaning, and meaning attracts effort. Meaning *deserves* effort.

Project-based homeschooling is built on a strong foundation of self-motivation. All project work is self-motivated because it is self-chosen. Your child is pursuing his own interests and his own goals. You don't have to coax him to do the work — it's exciting and meaningful from the start. You simply help him focus on what he wants to do, and you help make it significant and challenging.

Humans learn best when they are self-motivated. They learn best when they feel their chosen task is meaningful and important and worth their time. This is true for adults as well as children. Besides offering the best-possible environment for building thinking and learning skills, working on something real helps a person learn about himself: what he cares about, what he enjoys, what makes him come alive.

Research

> Research: *the systematic investigation into and study of materials and sources in order to establish facts and reach new conclusions.* — Oxford American Dictionary

> "That's what Hermione does. When in doubt, go to the library." — *Harry Potter and the Chamber of Secrets*

The nitty-gritty of investigation, research, experimenting, gathering information and opinions — what does this work look like when it is done by children? How can we create an environment that encourages self-directed investigation?

Projects start by discussing what we already know — or what we think we know. We start by talking to the people closest to us (family members, friends) and asking questions, listening to personal stories. As we gather new information, we make plans, list questions, share ideas. Slowly, we begin to talk to people outside our immediate circle. As our questions become more detailed, we seek out information from librarians, professionals, experts.

Everything we do is aimed toward increasing our understanding. Our ideas move the project forward — what we know, what we don't know, what we can build, what we can do with what we build, who we can talk to, who we can ask, who we can tell, how we can show them what we've learned.

things you might do

Make a list of what you think you already know.

Start a list of questions to answer. Hang it on the wall.

Invite friends and family to share stories and artifacts.

Brainstorm places where you might find more information.

Consider your options for gathering information. Ask your child, "Where do you think we could find out more about this?" *Always start with your child's ideas.* Encourage her to ask friends and family members to suggest possible sources (books, magazines, businesses, libraries, experts, online sources). Seek out help from knowledge gatekeepers (librarians, adults, peers, professionals). Read books, watch movies, talk to experts.

Don't skip this stage of research by doing it for your child. A pile of library books magically appearing jumps ahead in the learning process, and she'll lose the opportunity to experience sifting through the possibilities at the library and making her own choices. Let her think about what she wants to look for. Let her talk to the librarian on her own. Let her explore her choices and decide whether she found what she needed. Let her return again and again to refresh her resources.

Start at square zero, brainstorming places to find information and asking others for their suggestions. Each stage of learning is important — let your child experience them all. Let her control the

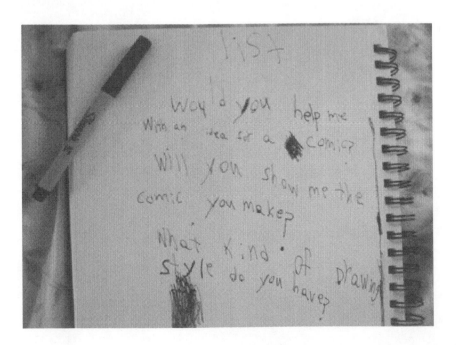

flow of information — choosing her own library books, choosing how many to bring home. If it's too much or too little, she'll figure it out. If a book seems too old for her, let her borrow it anyway. If it seems too young, don't discourage her. Encourage her to explore a variety of source materials. Let her compare their information, weigh their relevance, and decide what's more and less important. These are important steps you don't want to skip.

things you might do

Take your time at the library — explore everywhere.

Talk about what you'll look for before you go.

Make a list of questions you want to ask or things you want to look for.

Ask the librarians for help — encourage your child to do the talking.

Talk with friends and family and ask for their suggestions.

Make a list of all the places you want to visit, near and far.

Tackle each idea separately over time — don't rush.

Collect books, magazines, maps, and more in your workspace.

Display materials on your bulletin board — add photos of your child working.

Make blank books (folded and stapled paper) available.

Offer tools for keeping track of ideas: journal, sketchbook, clipboard, folders, posterboard.

You've found your first sources of information. Now you'll go out and gather facts and knowledge to bring home and work with.

This gathering happens at the source (e.g., selecting which books to bring home from the library) and again on a different level when you're back at home (e.g., choosing pages to photocopy and hang on your bulletin board, marking sections to read aloud together, drawing/painting/sculpting/building models referring to photos in the books). There is a constant process of narrowing down — finding the answer to a particular question, deciding what to model or draw or sculpt, focusing on a particularly interesting detail. After that particular part of the project has been explored to your child's satisfaction, she moves on to the next most interesting or relevant bit. In this way, she builds understanding — working to achieve competence and then moving on to fresh territory.

things you might do

Build up a project library — gather your materials together in your workspace.

Select things to read or have read aloud. Mark pages with sticky notes.

Take a lot of notes. Use homemade books, clipboards, sticky notes, etc. Pre-readers can make notes by drawing pictures.

Copy interesting book pages and hang them on your bulletin board.

Investigate encyclopedias. Talk about how they're organized.

See if you have project-related material in your own home library. Bring it into your workspace.

Make observational sketches. Always have clipboards and pencils with you.

Collect project-related ephemera: maps, magazines, pamphlets.

Label drawings; have pre-readers dictate parts to label.

Do observational drawings of artifacts, hang up the sketches, then make three-dimensional models.

For early writers, make lists of illustrated project vocabulary words that they can refer to and copy if desired.

You won't just gather information from books — you'll also collect real-life items related to your topic. You want a collection of things that your child can hold, examine, sketch, draw, paint, model, sculpt, and study at leisure. Having daily access to specimens, tools, instruments, and samples will spark questions, enrich your children's representations, and enliven their dramatic play.

Useful artifacts include sample materials, borrowed equipment, clothing, tools, accessories — anything that is used in real life. For an ocean project, this might include seashells, starfish, jars of sand and salt water, an aquarium full of seaweed, a live crab, diving equipment, fishing equipment, and so on. These artifacts are collected (and sometimes donated or loaned by interested friends and family) over time, examined closely, drawn/painted/modeled, and possibly used for dramatic play.

Your child can compare and contrast these real-world articles with photos and descriptions from books, things she sees in movies and at museums, and more. She can compare them to each other. She can draw them, paint them, model them in clay, and build representations with recycled materials. She can sort them, categorize them, and label them. She can create an informational display for visitors or photograph them to make a book.

The more real-world materials your child can personally handle and examine, the better. But let the artifacts accumulate slowly over time, in an organic and meaningful way. Don't simply fill up a table with things *you* have chosen — let her build and curate the collection.

things you might do

Display and label artifacts and collections of samples.

Use open trays to keep things organized but still visible.

Use an aquarium to observe bugs and small creatures for awhile.

Keep drawing tools nearby: pencil, paper, clipboard, etc.

Photograph collections and make a book. Video them to make a film.

Keep investigative tools nearby: measuring tape, scale, tweezers, magnifying glass.

Keep field guides nearby, with sticky notes for marking pages.

Look for tools specific to your project: e.g., rock hammer, insect cages, sewing machine.

Make tools available for closely examining, comparing, measuring, and exploring collected artifacts and specimens. Your workspace can be a science lab, a nature study, an artist's studio, a woodworking shop, and more. No matter what work is taking place, take an investigative attitude.

things you might do

Measure specimens with measuring tapes, rulers, unifix cubes.

Weigh specimens on a scale.

Use magnifying glasses and microscopes to look close.

Use clipboards/dedicated notebooks for ongoing note-taking.

Offer tweezers, protective goggles, and other scientific equipment.

Provide test tubes, slides, specimen bottles and boxes.

Design your own experiments; take notes and photographs.

Compare drawings and models with those of a friend.

Identify your specimens with books and field guides and read about them.

Render your artifacts in a wide variety of media.

Representations

Your child represents his learning by making, and he learns *while* making. He not only makes two- and three-dimensional artworks, but he creates experiences — dramatic play, skits, songs, games, exhibitions, parties. He makes and creates not only to demonstrate what he knows, but to explore ideas and concepts — the process of creating a representation is a learning experience in and of itself.

Representations are not simply products — creating them is a crucial part of the learning process.

Your child creates models that spark questions that require research that helps him refine his ideas, then he goes back and improves his models. Questions uncover answers that lead to new questions. It is a spiral process of gathering information, using it to make something, uncovering new questions, gathering new information, and refining ideas.

The process of making contains an additional layer of learning. Your child learns about materials and what he can and can't do with them. He acquires skills in drawing and painting and sculpting and building and designing. He learns to plan and make first drafts, write lists of needed materials, and adapt materials to new uses. He solves many problems, from how to attach two heavy boxes together to what paint will stick to packing tape to how to best represent the skin of an alligator.

By expressing himself through his play and creating many different types of representations, he steadily builds understanding.

The more variety you can offer in raw materials, space, and opportunity to create different experiences — art, construction, dramatic play, music, theatre, puppetry, light and shadow play — the more you help your child learn and understand.

The products of your child's learning are representations of what he knows and what he needs. They have nothing to do with the feeble assigned activities that some educators tack on and call "hands-on" or "project-based." In a non-authentic project, children might be required to design a pretend ad campaign, write a pretend newspaper article, or videotape a pretend news broadcast. In authentic project work, the representations aren't pretend. They're real. They aren't assigned. Your child makes something genuine according to his own ideas and plans. He builds something because he wants it or needs it. He does real work for a real purpose.

Project learning produces knowledge, and focusing on meta-learning (learning how to learn) enhances skills. Knowledge and skills combine with your child's ideas to yield representations of his thinking and learning: drawings, paintings, books, posters, movies, blog posts, sculptures, models, skits, games.

Every project will not produce *all* of these things. Each project should produce original work that is meaningfully related to your child's investigations and what she wants to accomplish. A group of children will produce a large variety of representations because they each follow their own specific interests. If your child is working alone, she may focus on one particular way of representing what she's learning: for example, producing a series of stop-motion films. Even with that focus, she'll use many different skills to create one complex project — for example, creating a film may involve a lot of writing (creating scripts), drawing (storyboards), collaborating (enlisting friends as actors), and etc. But keep your expectations realistic. If your child is producing real, meaningful work that requires research, concentrated effort, problem-solving, and collaboration, support that work. She won't produce every possible kind of representation for every single project, and you shouldn't expect her to.

Authentic project work is genuine. It isn't coerced or assigned. It grows out of your child's ideas. It's rooted in what she's learning and thinking about. It isn't suggested or required — it's planned and designed by your child to meet her own goals. It isn't superficial busy work — it's meaningful work.

Two-dimensional works may be fanciful (e.g., free drawing, free painting, collaging stories, writing fiction) or observational representations (e.g., sketches from life, labeled drawings and plans for small or large three-dimensional models, notes from experiments). Both types of work should be encouraged.

things you might do

Drawings

Paintings

Observational sketches

Labeled blueprints and plans for constructions

Prints

Collages

Murals

Posters

Charts

Maps

Books

A fully stocked art studio that's always accessible is the best encouragement for working and creating. Your regular workspace can function as an art studio if materials are within reach and the surfaces are easy to clean. Plastic or canvas tablecloths and floorcloths can help turn your living space into a making space that accommodates the mess that's a byproduct of creativity.

Remember: Out of sight, out of mind. If art materials are put away in a cabinet or on a high shelf, children won't see them and therefore won't think as often about using them. Bowls, baskets,

Accommodate mess so your child can relax and create.

plastic jars, and shallow trays help keep things organized and in sight. Aesthetics are important — the more beautiful the space and the materials, the more likely your child will be to use them.

things you might do

Pencils — Pencil sharpeners — Colored pencils — Watercolor pencils

Markers, thin and fat, all colors including black

Ink and brayer — Recycled styrofoam for printmaking

Chalk — Pastels — Oil pastels — Charcoal

Old magazines/junk mail/found paper/copies of photos for collaging

Fabric scraps — Yarn scraps — Ribbon

Scissors — Glue — Glue sticks — Stapler — Highlighters

Office supplies of every sort — Sticky notes — Book rings — Fasteners

Cellophane tape — Masking tape — Duct tape — Foil tape

All types and sizes of paper including tissue paper — Paper scraps

Notebooks — Clipboard — Loose notebook paper — Easel paper

Watercolor paints — Watercolor paper — Watercolor pencils

Tempera paint — Acrylic paint — Fabric paint — Paintbrushes — Foam brushes

Small homemade blank books (fold and staple pages)

Easel — Paint cups with lids — Small safety mirror (for self-portraits)

Aprons (old button-up shirts worn backwards) — Old sheets or vinyl tablecloths to protect the floor

Three-Dimensional Representations

Your child can make three-dimensional representations from a variety of materials from play dough to air-dry clay to clean recycled materials.

Three-dimensional representations can be temporary (e.g., sandbox play, block constructions) as well as permanent. Take photos of ephemeral constructions and hang them up; your child might want to write about them, incorporate the photos into books as illustrations, or remake them in a more permanent form.

All kinds of "junk" can become a three-dimensional sculpture or model. Plastic lids, nuts and bolts, bits of packaging — collect these together and let them spark your child's imagination.

Clean recyclable materials can be used for making constructions and recycled later on. Save foam trays for print-making, wrapping paper for collaging, and so on.

A wide variety of materials beautifully displayed attracts and inspires.

Very large constructions can be made using cardboard, inexpensive lengths of fabric, or newspaper rolled and taped together into a framework.

Outdoors, your child can put natural materials to use. Consider collecting pinecones, sticks, sawn sections of tree limbs, pods and dried flowers, interesting pebbles and rocks, and similar materials and keeping them near the sandbox or garden for building and constructing. Display some of these materials in your art studio as well — for indoor art making and block building.

All sorts of ordinary household items can be used as tools for shaping clay, play dough, and similar materials (outdoors: mud, sand, and snow). Save old kitchen utensils, junk-mail credit cards, and the like and experiment with them.

things you might do

Three-dimensional models

Clay sculptures (play dough, air-dry clay, modeling clay)

"Junk" sculptures from clean recyclables (cardboard and more)

Woodwork — balsa and glue or hammer and nails

Cardboard dollhouses and other buildings

Clay relief — carved designs and/or poked-in materials

Soap and plaster carvings

Mud and plaster casts of footprints or homemade molds

Small constructions (e.g., block scenes, tabletop models)

Large constructions (child-size vehicles, furniture, and play scenes)

Weavings

Papier-mâché

Wire forms

Costumes

Stuffed fabric forms

Stuffed paper forms

Tyvek or heavy paper sewn or joined with duct tape

Masks and costume accessories

Props for dramatic play

Three-dimensional materials can take up a lot of room. Display small items in your studio or workspace in jars, bowls, baskets, or trays. Flatten large cardboard boxes when not in use and store them; once they can no longer be reused, recycle them. Keep a selection of medium-sized clean recyclables on hand (cardboard boxes and tubes, plastic lids, foam trays, etc.), and if your child needs more, ask friends or neighbors. Be creative with what you offer — your child's imagination will delight in a wide array of different types of materials.

things you might do

Cardboard boxes — Cardboard tubes

Clean recyclables with no sharp edges

Plastic bottles — Lids — Caps

Styrofoam — Sheets of cardboard — Found papers

Fabric — Yarn — Ribbon — Buttons

A collection of clean recycled boxes, tubes, and other miscellaneous building materials make three-dimensional modeling easy.

Pipe cleaners — Wire (be careful — wire ends can be sharp)

Cotton balls — Pom-poms — Sequins — Decorative scraps

Popsicle sticks — Balsa wood — Wood scraps — Wood glue

Masking tape — Cellophane tape — Duct tape — Craft tape

Play dough — Modeling clay — Air-dry clay — Clay tools

Tempera paints — Acrylic paints — Watercolors — Fabric dye

Older Children and Teens

Your child's workspace can be an art studio, a film-making studio, a science lab, a nature study, a business office, a library, a music studio.

Create a rich environment for creating and expressing ideas. Your child might write music about the animals he's studying at the nature preserve or make films about space exploration. The learning happens in two directions — taking information in and creating something to share wth others.

The older child or teen can build on his previous making experiences and do much more. Check your library for books to inspire new ideas.

things you might do

Films — Stop-motion — Claymation — Brickfilms — Videos

Theatrical skits — Plays — Performances — Songs — Stories

Screen-printing — Fabric dyeing — Batik — Raw wool

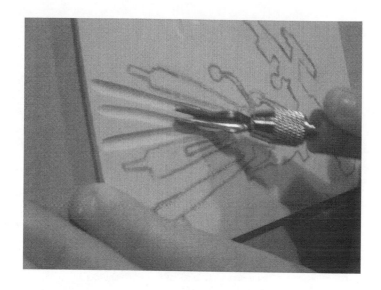

Designing T-Shirts, Bags, CD packaging, Books, Journals

Weaving — Sewing — Knitting/Crocheting — Embroidery — Macramé

Clay sculpture — Pottery — Jewelry design — Leatherwork

Print-making — Print carving — Glass and metal etching

Cartoons — Comics — Comic books — Graphic novels

Books — Stories — Poems — Scripts — Storyboards

Brochures — Posters — Booklets — Maps — Charts

Websites — Blogs — Shared blogs — Photo blogs — Podcasts

Newspapers — Newsletters — Letters/e-mails to experts

Computer programs — Video games — Board games

Models — Sculptures — Displays — Exhibitions

Photographs — Artwork — Art shows — Art clubs — Art walks

Scientific experiments — Nature study

Fieldwork

Visit places in the community where you can learn about aspects of your project: businesses, manufacturers, museums, libraries, public exhibitions, art galleries, shows, demonstrations, collections, parks, nature preserves, universities. Visit people in the community who might share their knowledge: experts, specialists, collectors, professionals, amateurs, interest groups, classes, clubs.

Always start by asking your child, "Where do you think we could learn more about this? Where do you think we could see this in person?" Take his ideas seriously and follow up. If he has no ideas, encourage him to ask other people for suggestions. You've heard the expression "make short work of this" — always make *long* work of it instead. At every stage of the project, start by talking it over and exploring your child's ideas. Let him make the suggestions; let him make the plans.

Fieldwork is his opportunity to see how his project connects with your community and the real world. You need to make this connection regardless of what your child is studying.

Keep an open mind and look for ways to make the exotic accessible. If you can't visit a pirate ship or an ocean liner, see what boats are used locally and for what purpose. If you can't go to outer space, you can still visit the planetarium and maybe an air and space museum. Look for ways to put the faraway within reach. If you can't visit the jungle, you might be able to see a monkey at your local zoo and a palm tree at the arboretum. If your child wants to study tigers, he can read about them and possibly see one at the zoo (hopefully more than once), but he can also study your family cat up close and make all the necessary comparisons and contrasts. Break a project topic down into its elements and think about where you might look at its component parts. Always ask others for their suggestions — they might lead you to exciting opportunities you'd otherwise miss.

Encourage your child to voice his own ideas and ask other people for their suggestions — don't simply schedule fieldwork and produce it as a fait accompli. Let your child do the useful work of asking for suggestions, weighing options, choosing a location, finding out when

they're open, anticipating what will happen there, and planning what to bring along. Help him e-mail ahead to make appointments with experts, then make a list of questions to ask. Strongly consider returning at least once, if not more — multiple visits to the same site produce the richest results.

things you might do

Always bring clipboards and pencils — sketch everything.

Take photographs of what your child sketches.

Take photos of your child working.

At home, label observational drawings and display them with the photos.

Let your child take photographs and video.

Collect ephemera from places you visit — let your child display and categorize it.

Before doing fieldwork, talk about what you expect to see and do. When you return home, discuss how the reality met up with your child's expectations.

Interview experts — bring prepared lists of questions.

Collect samples — bring empty plastic bags and jars.

Brainstorm about what you see that you might build at home.

Bring a friend along.

Take your time — plan to visit more than once.

Play: Exploring and Using Ideas

It's not enough for your child to study and memorize facts. In order for him to really explore something and internalize what he learns, in order to really understand it, he needs to do what children do best: play.

Play is a way for children to try on ideas and see how they work. It's a way to increase understanding by trying on adult roles and dramatizing adult situations. It's also a way for older children and teens — and adults — to explore new ideas in a relaxed way that enhances perception. No matter what age you are, playing with new ideas helps you understand them better.

In a year-long ocean project, a group of three- to five-year-olds made a large group of representations including three-dimensional fish and other sea creatures (octopus, shark, jellyfish, etc.) and diving equipment (goggles, oxygen tanks, flippers, etc.). They painted a large mural of undersea life. The sea creatures and fish were hung from the ceiling in front of the mural, and the children would wear the diving equipment they'd constructed and pretend to swim amongst the sea creatures they'd made. While they swam, they talked about what they knew about the sea creatures, working those facts into their play. They were oceanographers, they were divers, they were sharks and eels. With small children, it's impossible to separate learning and play — they're woven together.

Children studying the library might visit the library, make sketches of things they see there, write or dictate notes in their journals, take photographs, etc., then return home to construct their own library complete with props like date stamps, computer, card catalogs, etc. They can play with their homemade props, acting out the adult roles they observed. Through this kind of play, they express what they've learned and at the same time explore what they may not understand. If you're observant, you can use their play to identify questions that still remain, find confusions or disagreements that can be rephrased as questions, and recognize connecting ideas that the children are discovering. Write these observations down and bring them up later as prompts for further work.

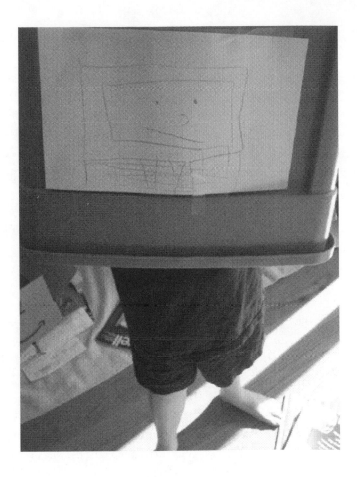

Never think that "playing" doesn't count as real learning, no matter how old your child is. Play enhances learning. Play reinforces learning. Play is how your child begins to use what he knows in a real way. Play is how children learn.

When your child makes a sculpture of a frog, he can show what he's learned and what he understands about frogs so far; he can show his clay frog to someone and explain the knowledge it represents. But when he takes that clay frog and makes a world for it to inhabit — a home, a habitat, food — and then becomes deeply involved in imagining its life and its routines and how they connect to himself and his own life, then he is learning in a very complex and powerful way, through play.

A child might draw a book about firefighters, then make his own badge and hat by carefully following photos in books or sketches from a field trip. When he uses those props to *become* a firefighter — reinforcing through role-playing everything he knows about how firefighters work and live as well as imagining how it must feel to be a firefighter — then he takes his learning to a deeper level. He uses play to explore ideas and increase his understanding.

Play is not the opposite of work — it's the *way* children work. It's an important step in allowing children to use what they know.

Instead of just displaying models and constructions on a shelf, encourage your child to play with them. They can use sculptures and models in combination with other open-ended playthings (dress-up fabric, blocks, play furniture). The more they play, the more they explore ideas and concepts. The more freedom you give children to use what they make for imaginative play, the more they'll learn and understand.

Play is the universal learning medium. — Vivian Paley

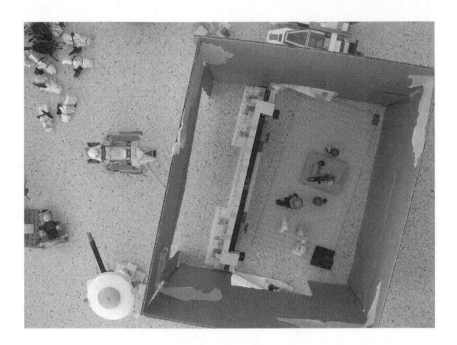

Play is the best way of extending work and deepening understanding — and the best way to spark new questions.

Play is intense interaction with ideas and feelings. It uncovers new questions and reveals confusions. It gives a direction to future project work. And it's fun.

Models can be repaired or rebuilt if necessary; just remember to take photos of completed work before you allow it to be well and thoroughly used. The process of fixing damaged constructions can inspire children to extend and improve on their earlier design. Use everything — don't let any opportunity to engage go to waste.

Remember that children can project-play indoors and outdoors if they have the space, the opportunity, and your encouragement.

Dramatic Play: Creating and Controlling Worlds

Children need space in which to "work large" — space that is big enough and flexible enough to become anything they want it to be: a doctor's office, a science lab, a grocery store, a film studio, a zoo, an aquarium. If space is available, their work and their play will grow to fill it. In a small space, they might build tabletop models; in a large space, they can build a rocket big enough to play in.

Ideally, this space should be located adjacent to their art materials/workspace so they can associate what they make with how they can use it.

In this open and flexible space, they can create models and props, make costumes, build large constructions, and integrate what they make with generic items that can be repurposed for their play. Empty space is full of possibilities.

If possible, let your child have space to leave constructions out so they can be added to and worked on over days or weeks. They can achieve a much greater complexity of detail if they can return again and again to the same representation or dramatic play scene. If it's in a place of honor with space to work and play each day, they can take their ideas further. They can layer on more ideas, more learning.

Children may use existing open-ended materials like blocks to create constructions related to their topic, integrating materials they make from scratch. Good open-ended construction materials allow children to integrate their own handmade items (clay figures, signs, models) to create many different worlds. They might make an airport or zoo out of blocks to house the planes or animals they've made out of clay, adding handwritten signs. Often, block constructions give children ideas for more permanent structures they'd like to build.

things you might do

Clear a large open floor space for dramatic play possibilities.

Empty space can become anything your child wants it to be.

Try to make permanent space for things like block play so your child can add to constructions over many days.

Permanent open play space means scenes can grow in complexity over time.

Open shelving for projects-in-progress reminds your child of his work.

If play space is adjacent to art/making space, your child will be more likely to combine and connect: adding handmade signs to block constructions, making props for dramatic play, etc.

Offer flexible, open-ended materials (large boxes, squares of fabric).

Combine homemade props with blocks and with dramatic-play materials.

Let children repurpose items and move them to new areas.

Keep reference books and bulletin boards near art-making and play areas for inspiration.

Follow project time with free time to avoid disrupting engagement.

Don't buy costumes and props — make them.

Open-Ended Materials

A large cardboard box can be anything a child wants it to be — car, train, boat, ticket booth, deli truck, post office counter.

Wooden, foam, or cardboard blocks can be used to build anything. Try to have as many of these open-ended materials available as possible; they hold much richer possibilities than rigid, can-only-be-used-one-way toys.

Try not to provide your child with too-specific props (e.g., a steering wheel); give him open-ended materials and let him build what he

needs himself. Learning opportunities are rich when a child has a set goal ("I need a steering wheel"), a set of problems ("How do I attach this?," "How can I make this round?"), and the chance to work out his own solution. This is where learning habits and dispositions can be exercised and developed: creativity (coming up with ideas), resilience (trying something else when a first attempt fails), communication (asking for materials), and so on.

Instead of purchasing specific dress-up clothes (e.g., a princess dress), provide a basket filled with squares and rectangles of different types of fabric (wool, lace, satin), ribbons, and other embellishments. Let the children do the work of creating their costumes from scratch. Hats, helmets, and props can be made in the art studio, with much thinking, planning, and problem-solving.

You can help your child sew or otherwise fasten together cloth or Tyvek to fashion special costumes with a sewing machine or using non-sew techniques like double-sided tape, fusible webbing (which only requires an iron), and even duct tape. (Duct tape is available in a rainbow of colors and even metallic finishes. It is strong, flexible, and long-lasting.) Tyvek can be decorated with permanent markers. You can even sew buttons and cut buttonholes. Tyvek envelopes can be recycled and cut into rectangles for sewing or art-making.

Children can even make fairly sturdy costumes from heavy brown paper — give them open-ended materials, then let them use their imaginations.

things you might do

Cardboard boxes can be flattened and stored when not in use.

A collection of fabric pieces can be used for temporary costumes (tied around the waist for skirts or aprons, over the shoulders for capes or bandanas, etc.) and props (tablecloths, curtains, etc.) or sewn into more permanent costumes.

Costumes can be created out of materials beyond fabric: heavy brown paper, recycled Tyvek envelopes, construction paper, tissue paper, etc.

Cardboard, heavy paper, and clean recyclables can be used to create hats, jewelry, and every kind of dramatic play prop. Pretend food and other props can be sculpted from air-dry clay, modeled with cardboard and tape, or sewn with felt and stuffed. Offer a wide variety of materials for your child to experiment with.

Take plenty of photos of large constructions and dramatic play spaces for documentation purposes. Take photos of your children playing in them — your child might use them to make books or displays, or looking at them might inspire new ideas.

Offer cameras and videocameras for your child to use or direct you to use. Children love to watch videos of their own dramatic play.

Between projects, clear everything out and let it be blank and generic again — a clean palette.

Group Work

There are many positive benefits in children working within a group. All shared work and play builds social skills — children negotiate to decide rules, share suggestions, and assign responsibilities. Working with others, especially toward a shared goal, adds another layer of possibility to project learning.

When you choose a project topic for a group of children, the interest must blossom from within the group. It doesn't have to be equally enthralling to every child from the outset, but there must be one or two children with a real passion for the subject and enough entry points for all the children to find something that interests them.

Children used to doing project work may decide to vote on what project topic to pursue next. Just as when you work with a single child at home, you may elect to collect project ideas by directly asking the children (soliciting suggestions and discussion) or by observing them during free art-making and play to identify strong interests.

When children work together — even siblings — it's important for them to learn to have respect for one another's work. For example, no child should ever draw or paint on another child's artwork without permission. Works-in-progress should be clearly labeled and treated respectfully. When children have disagreements about how to proceed with large, shared constructions, the adults in the room should help them learn to peacefully resolve their disagreements. Learning how to work together is one of the most important parts of project-based homeschooling.

Don't fall into the trap of thinking every child in your project group must be the same age. Children who range in age can work very well together, inspire one another, and enjoy both helping and being helped by their friends. Project work is self-leveling — children will naturally work at their own level, pursuing what interests them the most, sharing with the group, and learning from one another.

Ideally, you'll make sure that your child has the opportunity to experience working with both younger and older children rather than always being the youngest or oldest in the group. Your child should be able to experience all the important group roles over time: leader, supporter, expert, apprentice, teacher, student, collaborator, friend.

Older Children and Teens

It's not only small children who need the chance to play with ideas to fully understand them.

Younger children will engage in dramatic play. Older children and teens might organize skits or performances. They might devise exhibits and informational tours for friends and relatives. They might videotape each other or make a movie. They might create a stop-motion film studio, a screen-printing workshop, or a chemistry lab.

Older children play with concepts and ideas by using them to create something of their own. They make artwork: drawing, painting, sculpting, building. They might replicate experiments, from science to psychology. They can create useful materials to share what they know: brochures, posters, films, slideshows, websites, e-zines, blogs, wikis, books, podcasts, videos.

For older children and teens, think of playing as relaxed exploration. They need the opportunity to just mess around with what they're learning, with no firm aim or goal. Relaxed exploration is what sparks the ideas that lead to purposeful creation. Make sure they have the time, space, and materials for this. If their schedule is too full, they'll miss this important stage of improvising and experimenting.

You want to help your children go beyond taking information in and find a way to express themselves — what they know, what they believe, what they want to share. You take knowledge from the two-dimensional level to the three-dimensional level, working with it and making something new.

If, after a generous amount of "messing around" time, they settle on a goal — making a film, writing a book — they'll be able to work with focus and purpose.

With project-based homeschooling, we are always looking for a way to make our new knowledge useful — a way to share with our friends and family, a way to contribute to our community. We want to explain what we've learned and teach someone else. This is how we really know we understand something: when we can explain it to someone else. This is how we become a useful member of society: by contributing something useful and meaningful.

Talking about the Work

When They Are Working

Remember to let your child's ideas take precedence. Try to maintain a calm, open attitude and allow him to own his own excitement and interest.

Don't take over. Don't flood him with your own ideas; write them in your journal and save them for later. You may not need them, or your child may come to them on his own. Or, your child may have better ideas — ones you never anticipated. He may take his learning in an entirely unexpected direction. Keeping track of your own ideas can help you stay alert to possibilities, but make sure your child is focused on *his* ideas, not yours. Let him make the discoveries, and let him chart his own course.

If you have a particular thing in mind — an answer, an idea, a plan — then you may miss your child's idea, question, or plan. He'll figure out quickly that you're thinking of or fishing for a particular answer or response, and he will either stop driving the project and focus on pleasing you or shut down rather than offer up something he suspects may be wrong or not what you want. Create an environment where your child feels free to offer up all his ideas, questions, plans, and decisions and doesn't have to worry about meeting your expectations, reading your mind, or pleasing you. This is his work and he should be concentrating on doing it his way, to his own satisfaction.

If you regularly remind your child of his own plans and intentions, he'll internalize the habit. He'll begin to ask himself, "What was I going to do? What do I need to do next?" His environment can help: his bulletin board, his workspace, and his works-in-progress will remind him what he wanted to accomplish.

You encourage your child by being excited about his project, but don't make such a fuss that you distract him from his work and make it about your praise and approval. His focus should be on following his interest where it leads, not trying to please you or decipher where you wish it would go. If you project a relaxed attitude of enjoyment of learning, pleasure in being together, and certainty that things will get accomplished, he can relax and concentrate on his own feelings and aspirations.

You are defining your family values. You're communicating, "We work hard on things we care about. We enjoy them, and we share them. It's the way we live." You want this to be your ordinary way of life, in the best sense of the word — expected, everyday, automatic. You celebrate it by paying attention to it, sharing it, and savoring it.

When They Ask for Help

When she's working, it's inevitable that she'll become stuck, make a mistake, or become confused. Help her by modeling how to work through it rather than just giving her a solution. Don't straighten out her thinking for her — let her tease the knots apart by herself. Say, "What else could you try?" Say, "Where could you find more information?" Instead of offering up solutions, you are helping her get into the habit of seeking them for herself. You are showing her the steps she needs to take to begin to untangle her own confusion and correct her own mistakes.

Share your own frustrating experiences. Say, "I'm going to set this aside for awhile and then look at it again later. I can't figure it out. I might need to ask someone for help." Let your child see how you deal with ordinary frustration. Let her see you confront normal, everyday problems and work through them.

When she says "I can't," help her break her goal down into small, manageable tasks. For example, if she says "I can't draw a house!," walk her through it:

- Find a piece of paper.

- Think of what shape of house you want to draw.

- Look around the room at other things with the same shape.

- Do you want to draw our house?

- Let's go outside and draw while looking at it.

- Do you want to draw another kind of house?

- You can look through books for examples.

- We can take a walk around the neighborhood.

- Look at the house you are drawing. What do you see?

- What can you add to your drawing? What else does a house have?

Help her along until she gets back on track, then let her continue under her own steam.

A child who gets practice breaking down complex goals into smaller, more manageable tasks can apply that skill in other situations. As she experiences success, she'll approach new challenges more confidently.

You don't abandon your child to figure things out on her own, but you don't step in to fix her mistakes for her. You are her learning mentor — you show her the ropes and let her know you have faith in her abilities. You support her, but you expect her to do her own challenging work.

When They Are Wrong

If you see your child headed off in the wrong direction, don't jump in to correct him. Wrong turns can lead to great discoveries, and self-caught, self-corrected mistakes are more likely to be understood and remembered.

If your child is attempting to, say, attach a heavy wheel to a cardboard box with flimsy tape, let him try and fail. Several things might happen: one, you have jumped the gun and that was only the first part of his plan; two, he will figure it out himself and try something else and continue until he succeeds; three, he will become frustrated and you can step in to help him focus on trying other solutions. Each one of those scenarios is much more valuable than simply skipping over that part of the learning process.

Your child will always learn more by being allowed to make mistakes. He'll learn that not every idea is a great idea and first attempts are not always successful. He'll learn failure is just a temporary setback if you don't quit. He'll come to realize that mistakes are a part of doing anything significant. He'll get experience in what it's like to do real work: it's challenging, it doesn't always go smoothly, and it requires persistence. And a sense of humor doesn't hurt.

Be sure to call attention to the times when he successfully realizes a mistake, solves a sticky problem, or works past a temporary failure. Talk about what happened, what he did, what worked, and what

didn't. Share your own experiences, always. Let him know that everyone has these experiences, including adults, and we all have to work past them. Let him know you're proud of him for sticking with it and figuring it out.

When They Express Frustration

In *Being Wrong: Adventures in the Margin of Error*, Kathryn Schulz writes, "To err is to wander, and wandering is the way we discover the world." This is project-based homeschooling. To have a learning life centered on exploring and creating, we must allow for making mistakes. We are not concentrating on finding right answers or checking off boxes. We are jumping in feet first to do real, exciting work.

Expect mistakes and problems — they're a normal part of working and learning. Model resilience. Show a calm confidence that your child will find a way. Encourage him to step back and think about his options; if necessary, brainstorm with him. Give him the time and support to solve his own problems.

Talk about your own mistakes. During your normal day, articulate when you're disappointed and verbalize how you'll work through it.

Accept mistakes as an unavoidable part of learning. Let your child feel frustrated, but also let him see that his mistakes don't upset you. Help him move on. "Now we know what doesn't work. What should we try next?"

Don't do work for your child that he can do himself, just because he's unhappy with his level of skill. Say cheerfully that the more he draws, paints, sculpts, uses scissors, etc., the better he'll get. Expect him to improve with time. Let him know you're confident he'll master it with practice. When appropriate, pull out older samples of his work and let him see how his skills have improved.

Draw and paint and create alongside your child if the spirit moves you. Don't worry about being "better" than he is. Art skills are no different from skills like reading, writing, cooking, or driving. You aren't afraid your superior reading skills will make your child reluctant to read. You're so confident he'll become an expert reader,

you don't give it a second thought. Make sure he knows you feel that way about all of the thinking, learning, and making skills. Draw and paint together. Enjoy each other's company. Your competence will inspire, not inhibit him, especially if you communicate your confidence that he'll steadily grow as an artist, designer, and builder.

You can, of course, help a small child with things he's unable to do — say, cutting heavy cardboard. Simply be clear that you expect him to do his own work as well as he can, and you know he'll improve with practice.

A child who draws, designs, creates, and builds every day is more likely to feel confident and optimistic about his skills. The more practice he has, the more fluent he will become. The more it's a part of your ordinary routine, the more likely he is to be able to articulate his ideas the way he envisions them.

Praise

Avoid empty, nonspecific praise: "Great job." "Beautiful drawing." "Good work."

Make statements that describe your child as a powerful learner. "You really listened at the museum today, and you found the information you needed." "That was frustrating when the wheels fell off, but you didn't give up and you fixed it." "You talked to the librarian yourself today and remembered to bring your question list." "You've done so much work on your model this week. You've added a lot of detail."

Let your child talk about his work. Rather than praising him with words, show him with your actions how much you value what he's doing. Listen, pay attention, and always follow through when you make a promise.

Acknowledge his mistakes and make sure he sees that they help him work toward the right solution. Let him see that you're not bothered by failure and that you see it as a temporary setback. "What do you think went wrong?" "What are you going to try next?" "Let's make a list of other things you could try." "Which of your ideas do you want to try first?" Be relaxed so he can relax.

Be specific. "It wasn't easy to figure out how to connect those two pieces, but you thought of several good things to try and you did it." "Your poster really describes how your model works. Labeling the photographs was a great idea."

Be descriptive. "You added a lot of detail to your painting. You were patient to wait for the sky to dry before you painted the house." "The wire details on your model look very realistic. You worked hard to get it the way you wanted."

Avoid too much praise — it can be addictive and lethally distracting. Your child is doing his own meaningful, self-chosen work — it's inherently fulfilling. Let him experience the pleasure of doing that work apart from the idea of pleasing someone else or meeting their expectations. He should be defining his own goals and working toward meeting his own expectations.

Instead of praise, focus on building a family culture that appreciates, celebrates, and cultivates meaningful work through daily conversation, sharing, dedicating time to it, and giving it a place of honor in your home.

Encouragement

Help your child experience forward movement in his project. Help him stay with his own ideas. Remind him of his plans and make sure he has what he needs so he can fulfill his goals. "You asked for more black paint to finish painting your wheels; I have that for you now." "You asked if I would write down your story to go with the pictures you drew; I can do that this morning if you like."

After a project work period, talk about what he did and what he plans to do next time. Help him remember his plans the next time he comes back to his work.

With a group of children or siblings, have them share their work with one another and offer questions, comments, and suggestions. Take notes. At the beginning of the next project work period, remind the children of the plans and intentions they expressed last time.

Make sure your workspace supports your child's work and helps him remember what he wants to do. Write down questions on large sheets of paper and hang them on the walls; cross them off as the answers are found. Call attention to the progress he's made. Hang photos from a field trip next to sketches made there. Display material lists next to photos of a model in progress and, eventually, the finished model. Encourage your child to sit down and review completed work and reflect on what he's learned since he started his project. Every so often, reexamine the space and make sure it's neat, clean, and organized so that he can work independently.

When he's frustrated or angry about something that went wrong, don't cheerlead and don't become upset yourself. Project calm acceptance (things will always go wrong; it's inevitable) and optimism (you can always find another way; there's a solution somewhere). Suggest to your child that he can put his work away and look at it again tomorrow if he's not ready to try something else right away.

Using Questions to Start a Dialogue

Rather than making statements or suggestions, use open-ended questions:

- "Are you done with this?"

- "Is there anything more you want to do to this?"

- "Is there anything you need to finish this?"

- "What do you want to do next?"

- "What do you think?"

- "Who could we ask?"

- "Where could we find out about that?"

- "Did you find the information you needed?"

If you say, "You should do more with this," you're making the work about you and your expectations. If you say, "You never finished this like you said you would," you're nagging and turning project work into a chore. Remember: this is your child's own self-chosen work;

it's work he wants to do. Use questions to jumpstart conversations, help him remember his own ideas, and let him decide what to do and how.

Sharing Your Own Learning Experiences

Make your projects, your ambitions, and your triumphs and failures a normal part of family conversation. Let your child see that you're continuously learning, trying new things, brainstorming, correcting mistakes, working through problems, overcoming temporary failures.

Share your interests and passions. Tell your child stories; show her what you care about. Make sure your home reflects the interests, passions, and values of your family.

Share your thinking and learning strategies with your child. Let her see you think, consider possibilities, ponder choices, weigh options. Talk about your problems and how you plan to approach and resolve them.

Every time you talk with your child — every time you talk within your child's hearing — you have the opportunity to underscore your family's values for thinking, learning, working, and making.

How to Be a Mentor

You are your child's first and best example of a successful thinker and learner. You're mentoring him to acquire the skills and habits he needs to become an expert learner himself.

Your life doesn't have to be perfect. Let him see you react to disappointments and inevitable mistakes and deal with them. Set an example of resilience and perseverance.

Focus on the habits of mind that you most want your child to acquire and make them your priority. He'll absorb the lesson of what you *do* much better than what you *say*.

Talk it out — discuss what you're doing and why. Wonder out loud. Consider alternatives out loud. Express frustration, but follow it up with how you'll deal with the problem. Let him see you — and

hear you — as you work out your problems and work toward your goals.

Model good dispositions and useful attitudes. Take time to express delight and curiosity. Slow down. Set aside more time for errands and adventures — time to pause, reflect, ask questions, pay attention.

Let your daily life reflect your deepest interests, your passions, and your purpose. Surround yourself with things that remind you of what you most want to do with your day — and your life. Talk about your goals. Share your pleasures.

Hopefully, everything you want for your child, you also want for yourself: intellectual curiosity, playful learning, passion, and purpose. Let your life reflect your values, because your child will take his most serious lessons from the way you live.

things you might do

Wonder aloud.

Express delight and interest.

Devote time to your interests. Invest in yourself.

React to problems by considering alternatives out loud.

Voice disappointment, but follow up by voicing determination.

Ask pertinent questions and make meaningful suggestions.

Share your enjoyment in your own work.

Don't hide your mistakes — model resilience.

Share your passionate interests with others.

Reflect on your own accomplishments.

Ask for help when you need it. Offer help when you can.

Follow through with what you say you'll do.

You can help your child identify his own questions by helping him rephrase his wonderings, uncertainties, and confusions as queries. If he wonders out loud, says he doesn't know something, or has a disagreement with a friend or sibling, you help him reframe his uncertainty as something he can investigate — something that he can figure out with your help.

Maintain an ongoing list of questions. Gently remind your child about his intentions, and ask whether he's satisfied that he's found his answers and achieved his goals.

things you might do

Keep a question list — poster-size is good.

Until it becomes a habit, remind him to add new questions to the list.

Jot notes in your journal about things he wonders about.

Pay attention to conversation during meals and with friends.

When the project slows down, remind him of his own ideas and plans.

For pre-readers, regularly read the question list together.

Remind him of what he wants to know.

Help him turn disagreements or confusions into puzzles to investigate.

Keep ongoing projects front and center — don't hide them away.

Display his works-in-progress to remind him of his goals.

Take time often to reflect on what he's accomplished so far.

Start each project work period by reviewing what he wanted to do next.

End each project work period by recording his plans for next time.

Next time, remind him of his own plans and intentions.

Your child can build up a significant understanding if he collects enough related knowledge and has enough related experiences. Give him as many connected, project-meaningful pieces to work with as possible.

Keep a gentle but persistent focus on the project. Help him stick with his interest longer, explore further, and express his ideas in several different ways. Let books, artifacts, and representations accumulate. Don't distract him. Let him stay with his interest as long as he wants.

Help your child relate things that he reads, sees, hears, watches, discusses, visits, observes, etc., with one another. Use your walls and shelves and his workspace to display the parts of his project — what he's reading and looking at as well as what he's producing. Encourage him to mix, combine, and connect.

things you might do

Create a workspace that mirrors his work back to himself.

Keep things gathered in one place — sort and reorganize as you go.

Don't let one-off events derail his concentration and interest.

Make field trips project-relevant. Follow through on his ideas.

Schedule non-project-related events for between projects.

Take your time during fieldwork — let him work at his own pace.

Go back and repeat experiences.

Don't suggest new ideas until he's completely finished — don't distract.

Give him as many connected experiences and resources as possible.

Reflect often by reviewing journals, looking at bulletin boards, and reexamining the work he's produced (books, representations, models).

Respect the natural ebb and flow of focus. Let him think and dream.

When work slows or stops, mine your journal for his unfinished ideas.

Invite friends and family over and let him explain his work to them.

To help your child become an independent, confident thinker and learner, you need to help him develop strategies and habits that will support him along the way. Remember that every choice you make has an impact on your child's attitudes toward his abilities, his ideas, and his work. From his workspace and materials to your daily routine to how you talk about your life, your choices let him know what you value.

Deepening the Work

You've set the stage for doing challenging, meaningful project work with depth and dimension.

It's meaningful. The work is placed squarely in the context of your child's deep interests and natural talents.

It's shared. Your child collaborates and shares with your family, with friends, and with members of the community.

It's long-term. There's time for unhurried exploration, time to explore connections, time to think and dream, time to add to complex representations and constructions over many weeks.

It's complex. He has a generous variety of materials for making representations, a number of related experiences, and he's encouraged to explore his ideas in multiple ways.

Now you work to help him get beyond the superficial mode of learning that just skates around on the surface and then moves on to something else. You slow down, dig deep, and reflect thoughtfully. You challenge him to ask himself what else he can do. You help him set goals and work toward them. You loop back again and again, checking to see what he's accomplished and what else he wants to do.

By paying attention, by listening, and by mirroring back to him his own questions, thoughts, and ideas, you encourage him to turn his thoughts into action. He not only learns about his interests — he makes something real with his knowledge and his skills.

You help him build on his questions and ideas, and you look for ways to make the learning process more complex. You encourage him to explore further. You create an environment in which he feels free to challenge himself.

Getting Beyond the Surface of Learning

Imagine you are a child visiting the airport for the first time. You are excited by and interested in everything you see. You are riding a moving sidewalk that glides slowly past several different areas. You look at everything with interest as it rolls by. Finally, you disembark and go home. You tell your family about it at dinner, very excited. The next day, you are on to something else. You forget about the airport.

Digging deeper means forgoing one-off experiences and concentrating on having several *related* experiences. It means staying with one idea for a long time and exploring it thoroughly.

Fired up with excitement, questions, and ideas, you stay with that topic longer and dig into it more deeply. It becomes the focus for all

your intellectual energy. You unleash your curiosity. You immerse yourself in exploring it with all five senses and representing what you are learning in a multitude of ways.

Now, imagine that instead of moving on to something new, you get to go back to the airport. What new things might you notice? What new questions might you have?

Between trips, you had access to books about planes and airports and abundant materials for making two- and three-dimensional representations. You referred often to photographs and sketches from the first trip. You built a sprawling airport from blocks and populated it with planes you made from cardboard, clay, and plastic. You created airport workers and tools and vehicles. You used large cardboard boxes to build a plane cockpit you could really sit in. What if, on this next trip, you could draw and photograph a small plane up close? What would happen when you return to your work?

Too often, children have one-off, stand-alone experiences that don't really go anywhere. Those stand-alone experiences are like that one-way trip on the moving sidewalk. Your child gets to see a lot of interesting things, but he doesn't get to pause. He doesn't get to stop and really examine something closely. He doesn't get to hit reverse, go back, and look again. He might ask a few questions and get answers, but he doesn't get to follow a trail of inquiry that leads to more complex questions. He doesn't get to do anything with what he's learned. He doesn't get to ponder at length while he builds and makes and creates. He doesn't get the chance to combine his interest with his play.

Some adults attempting project-based learning make the same mistake, moving forward relentlessly and forgetting the importance of doubling back. Interests are identified, research is completed, and then there is a big, impressive third act that brings everything to a close.

Unfortunately, though appealing in its simplicity, this highly controlled approach cheats children out of the opportunity to lay down multiple layers of learning. The adult is satisfied. Is the child?

Adults are in a hurry. They like work to be linear and organized. They like planned outcomes. They enjoy making lists and checking

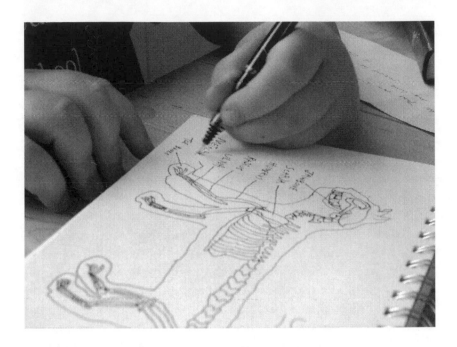

each item off. They like to tsk-tsk over children and their short attention spans, even when they themselves get bored almost immediately when a child wants to linger.

We need to curb our desire for getting things done and commit to the slow learning children need.

Deep, complex, inquiry-based investigation doesn't identify a single set of questions that are swiftly and neatly answered. Each new answer creates new questions, triggering new spurs of inquiry. It is this repeating cycle of questions and answers that leads children to collect a large amount of interrelated knowledge and build authentic understanding.

Rather than having a single beginning, middle, and end, good projects contain many beginnings, middles, and ends. Each line of inquiry is like a mini-project. Some investigations may be coming to a close while others are just beginning. If you are working with a group of children, they will change roles and focus throughout the project, so that some of them will just be beginning what others have already finished.

Rather than following a linear path, your child repeatedly loops back to the beginning, creating a spiral of learning.

Authentic projects are complex and layered. Some parts of the project have been thoroughly investigated and detailed representations are being constructed, but another part of the project is just blossoming as initial questions are formulated. New connections are continually being made; new insights are continually being discovered.

Children are allowed to wander, to approach the things that interest them, to double back for another look and maybe another, uncovering connections and making new discoveries along the way.

Tracing the same path over and over — each time with more knowledge, experience, and comprehension — builds not only understanding but also confidence. Your child is practicing his thinking and learning skills. Each time he returns to an experience and asks more of himself, he is working at a deeper and more challenging level.

Rather than learning the same tired handful of common facts about a subject (and soon forgetting them), your child digs beneath the surface to learn exciting new things that not everyone knows — things he can then share with his friends and family. Rather than remaining a novice, your child slowly acquires the understanding and authority of an expert.

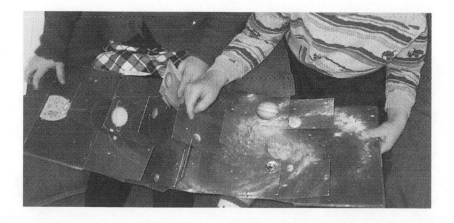

Setting The Pace

Project-based homeschooling is slow learning. Not in the sense of crawling along at a snail-like pace, but in the sense of generous amounts of unhurried, focused time over weeks and months. It requires patience. It requires an adult who really understands and appreciates the steps that go into building significant knowledge and authentic understanding.

This is creative work. Literally, your child is creating meaning, creating understanding, creating representations. She is building skills and knowledge from the raw materials of her project.

Creative work is nonlinear. It takes time. It takes detours and explores byways. It approaches ideas and problems from more than one direction. It doubles back for another look.

Creative work requires big chunks of unscheduled time. It requires freedom to explore, to try different things, to just think and imagine — and it requires a relaxed mindset. It is impossible to take your time and explore an idea in many different ways if you feel pressured by a lack of time or someone else's expectations.

The expectations should come from the one doing the work. And there should be plenty of unhurried time set aside to do that work.

Respecting your child's pace means not pushing her forward but also not artificially holding her back. You let go of your expectations and your plans and put her in charge of her own learning experience. She decides what she wants to do. She figures out how to do it. She decides when she's done; she decides if she's ready to move on or change her focus.

You help her remember her questions. You help her remember her goals. You help her keep track of her plans. You don't press her to move faster. You don't set an end date.

You gently encourage her to stick with her ideas, but you remember that she needs to learn to direct and manage her own learning. To do that, she needs experience in setting goals, making plans, and making decisions. You help her reflect on and assess her work, so she can judge whether she has made her best effort and reached her goals. But she gets to be the judge.

Your child defines her project with her questions, her goals, and her plans. To let her lead, you must let her go at her own pace.

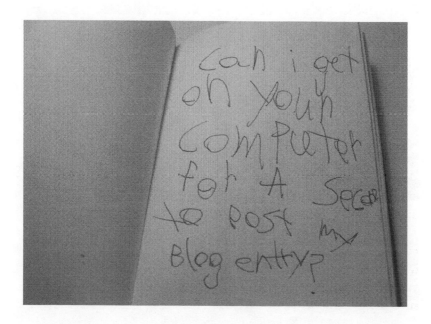

Extending Ideas

When your child completes a piece of work, don't assume she's done all she can do. Ask if there is anything else she wants to add. If she says yes, make notes and remind her during her next work period. If she says she doesn't want to work on it that day, respect the ebb and flow of authentic project work and set it aside, but return to it at a later date.

Use gentle prompts: "Is there anything else you wanted to add to this?" "Are you done with this?" "Do you want to display this?"

Encourage children to share ideas and ask questions about one another's work. Don't discourage one child from "copying" the work of another. The copier will usually add some new ideas, extending the first child's work. The originator is then often motivated to go back and add more to their first attempt (or start anew), often copying the copier. In this way, children working together can inspire each other to keep making the work more complex and detailed. They take turns having new ideas. The longer they stay with their work

and the more details they add, the more they deepen their understanding. They both end up with a more complex representation and more complete understanding because they continually challenge one another.

Encourage children to make suggestions to one another, but don't force them to take those suggestions. Allow children to own their work. Model polite acknowledgement and gentle refusals.

Going back and doing things again is a great way to encourage children to extend their work. You may wish to repeat fieldwork opportunities several times. Each time the children revisit the grocery store, fire station, or aquarium, they will find something they missed before. They will have new questions. They will notice more specific details. They will check the work they've done before and possibly make it more exact. Do special activities (e.g., working with high-quality clay, print-making) multiple times. Each time, the children will bring more experience, higher expectations, and more deliberate effort to the table.

Don't try to make your child's work easier. Don't try to smooth over his problems. The sticky spots are where he is learning the most. He is learning concrete facts about what materials can and can't do and which facts fit his theory, but he's also acquiring habits of mind and developing valuable qualities: resourcefulness, imagination, persistence.

things you might do

Keep work front and center so children remember their plans.

When work stalls, set it aside for awhile and bring it out again later.

Respect the natural ebb and flow of self-directed work.

Ask, "Are you finished with this?" or "Is there more you want to do with this?"

Write down your child's plans and intentions so you can help her remember later if she forgets.

Schedule time to look through your notes so you don't forget to reflect on and use the information you've gathered.

If your child asks for specific materials or assistance, make sure you follow through.

Encourage children to work together and share ideas, but don't force collaboration.

Respect the child who wants to work alone but ask him to share his work with others and ask for comments, questions, and suggestions. Find a variety of ways he can be part of a larger community.

Let him decide whether he wants to add to or extend his work.

Children working together need to learn to negotiate. Help them work through those first difficult debates to reach a fair resolution.

Don't discourage "copying." Let children add to, extend, and refine each other's work and ideas.

Revisit fieldwork opportunities and activities so children can notice things they missed before, repeat work with new information, etc.

Children can keep an interest going for a very long time — let them!

Expressing the Same Idea in Multiple Ways

If your child has done a very detailed drawing of a red-tailed hawk in his notebook, bring out new materials and let him rework it in different ways — with watercolor, with charcoal on large paper, with acrylic paint, as a collage.

Have his original works available for reference as well as research materials like books, posters, films, and photographs. A large variety of research materials allows him to compare and contrast. Making his representations, he will focus on examining his subject and finding details — this spurs him to ask deeper questions. He shows what he knows, and he works toward a deeper level where he needs to learn more so he can show more.

When he has done several renderings in two dimensions, bring out his drawings and paintings and set them beside three-dimensional materials like clay, recycled materials, and papier mâché.

The more he explores his idea through different media and different approaches, the more he will learn.

Keep track of the timeline of his representations. Take time to reflect together and talk about his progress. How are his later works different from his original drawings? What did he add/change? What changed when he moved to three dimensions? Help him see the progression of his own learning, how much more he learned and understood as he continued to investigate and layer on more detail.

Once your child has explored an idea in one way, encourage him to continue exploring that same idea in new and different ways.

things you might do

Repeat a drawing with a different medium.

Turn a drawing into a painting or vice versa.

Turn two-dimensional sketches into a 3-D model or construction.

Draw a labeled plan of a completed block structure or model.

Take photographs of completed constructions and label them.

Use costumes and props made for dramatic play to put on a skit for friends and family.

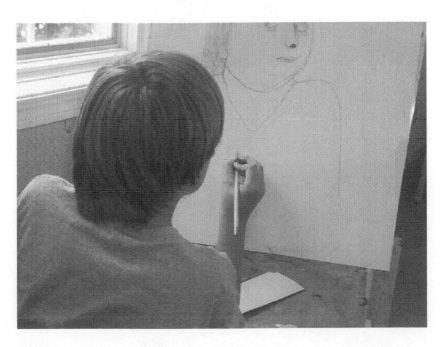

Bind loose artworks together, add words, and create a book. (Copy the originals if you prefer — make copies for friends, too.)

Make an exhibition out of completed models and representations and invite friends and family to visit. Prepare signage and brochures or booklets to explain the work.

Turn a series of photographs taken by your child into a book.

Make three-dimensional paper constructions of drawings.

Use photos of block constructions as artwork for a book, story, or poster.

How can you encourage your child to explore her ideas in different media without expressly suggesting it?

One, build up your child's vocabulary for expression. Between projects, explore new media. Take time to experiment in a relaxed and playful way with collage, watercolors, acrylics, weaving, sewing, clay, sculpting, modeling. Later, when your child's mind is full of her project work, interesting new facts, questions, and ideas, she will turn to these methods of expression and use them to say something meaningful. She'll use them to delve into her interest and come up with different ways of looking at it and saying things about it.

Two, use juxtapositions to provoke ideas. Set out materials with reference works and then step away. Make her workspace or studio a place full of possibility. If she is studying her goldfish, set up the watercolors in front of the bowl, but leave her to notice them and use them only if she wishes. If she has done a series of watercolor paintings on a particular subject, bring out the acrylics, a pile of heavy paper, and a large canvas. Combine her research materials with a place that invites making, and let her discover her own ideas.

Always apply the lightest touch possible. First, create an environment that is attractive and full of materials that beg to be used. Then support your child's interest, her questions, and her plans. Arrange things in an interesting, provocative way. Ask questions rather than making statements. Offer rather than suggest. Be patient and

wait for her to decide what she wants to do. Don't rush to fill empty space with your words or your suggestions. Make a space and a routine that encourage investigation, exploration, and creative making, then leave space for her ideas to grow.

Repeating Experiences

Your child wants to learn about cars, so you take him outside and open up the doors, hood, and trunk of your car and let him sketch to his heart's content. He draws, he paints, and he makes small models of cars out of clay and then recycled materials. Eventually he uses his sketches to make his own child-scale car out of cardboard and recycled materials: a car he can actually sit in.

Bring him out and let him sketch again. Date his sketches and compare them. Talk about them. How are they different? What new things did he notice? What new details did he add? How does this affect his construction? Does he extend his work by adding these new details?

Every time you repeat an experience, the place and the object may be the same, *but your child has changed*. He is bringing a new focus and asking new questions. He is looking at a deeper level. If you never repeat experiences, he never gets the chance to dig below the surface. Make sure he has the opportunity to work at that deeper, more complex level.

things you might do

Repeat observational drawings.

Repeat field trips.

Repeat visits to places in the community.

Contact an expert again with new, more detailed questions. Ask, "If you could talk to that person again, what would you ask now?"

Repeat opportunities to paint/sculpt/build/do special art activities.

Each new iteration allows your child to build upon what he already saw and understood and helps him create a deeper, more complex understanding.

Doing Multiple Drafts

When a drawing is finished or a model has been made from clay or cardboard or wire, adults have a strong inclination to check that box and move on to something new. New is not always better. Rather than a new experience or a new representation, consider instead a new iteration.

Try to put yourself into a different frame of mind. Creating multiple drafts of the same work allows your child to raise his efforts to a level that isn't possible if he simply creates first drafts over and over again. Rather than thinking about new versus old, consider the importance of an artist or craftsman revising and polishing their

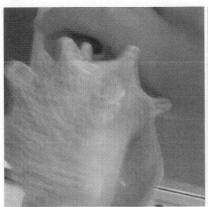 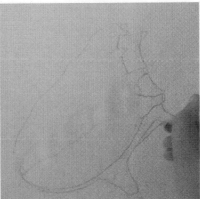

work, introducing improvements at each pass. Think about first and final drafts — and how much the work improves between them.

Not only does this process create work that is more thought out and more representative of what your child knows and wants to express, it gives him valuable experience in editing and polishing his ideas.

Each new pass allows your child to introduce new connections and more complexity, as his range of knowledge expands throughout the project.

He can bring new ideas and realizations back to his original idea and enhance it, extend it, improve it.

He learns that knowledge and thinking are flexible. Rather than arriving at one conclusion and setting it in stone, new information can be added to make the first attempt better. Over time, as more data is collected, thinking becomes clearer. He can see that the amount of effort he makes directly affects the quality of what he produces.

Multiple drafts also reveal the rich possibilities of mining just one vein of work. Initially, your child may create a rather simple drawing. As he accumulates more information, his drawing may become more complex. When he moves to three dimensions, new problems (and opportunities) arise as he works in a new medium.

When other children work alongside and create their own versions, ideas are shared, copied, and extended. He can attack the same problem in several different ways, digging down deeper with each version.

Creating representations is about communicating, and doing multiple drafts allows your child to get closer to what he wants to say.

When your child makes a drawing or a three-dimensional model, he is striving to communicate what he knows. He can work out his questions and his confusions with his hands, while he literally builds understanding.

When something doesn't work — when a material doesn't do exactly what he intended, when an idea fails — he can either quit in frustration or break it apart and try again. Your job is to gently encourage him to reconsider his options and think of a new solution. Creating multiple drafts means dealing with more mistakes and more problems, and it greatly increases the opportunities for learning.

With a slow pace, an open and inquiring mindset, and calm acceptance that problems are inevitable, we set the tone for a thoughtful approach to meaningful work. We begin to create a family culture that values interests, intellect, perseverance, resilience, and sharing.

Layering for Complexity

We are collecting a good supply of questions, experiences, knowledge, and representations. What can we do with them?

We increase the value of individual experiences by combining them to build something more complex.

Giving your child a lot of isolated, one-off experiences (say, with weekly themes or random field trips) is like giving her one plastic brick, one wooden block, one gear, etc. She has a handful of things to construct with, but what can she make? The pieces don't fit together. Your child can't combine them to make something meaningful.

Having a series of isolated, stand-alone experiences — a trip to the orchard, a visit to the planetarium, a day at the zoo — lets your child learn a little bit about several different things. She usually learns about them in the same way, too — she may visit a variety of locations, but the way she experiences them stays the same. Moving from one opportunity to the next, she never gets the chance to dig below the surface.

Having a series of experiences that connect meaningfully to one another allows her to begin to do more challenging intellectual work. A trip to the orchard, a visit to a local farm, interviewing the produce manager at the grocery store, back to the orchard, talking to the local extension officer, dissecting and sketching apples, planting an apple tree, going to the nursery, visiting a different orchard at the university — all of these experiences connect to one another. Your child compares and contrasts, she examines things closely and draws and models them, she asks questions, she seeks out answers from a variety of people, she interviews experts, she makes connections, and she puts ideas into action.

Children working together in a group will focus on different aspects of a project — the machines used to sort apples, the apples themselves, the trees, the tools, the jobs, the vehicles, the machines. They share what they learn with one another, so that each child in the group ends up with an understanding of each aspect of the project. They ask each other questions, make suggestions, copy one another's ideas, extend one another's work. They inspire one another with their intense interests and discoveries.

Whereas children in a group might focus on different aspects of the project and share them with each other, a child working alone might move from one focus to another over time. Each activity and experience connects to one main idea. That meaningful connection reinforces your child's understanding of each part and the complex whole.

By focusing on one authentic exploration that begins with your child's interest and travels outward along connecting lines of her investigation, you help her collect many building blocks that work together.

She will combine her knowledge and experiences to create a new and deeper understanding. She knows that these facts and experiences relate to one another. Now she can begin to explore how and why.

Collaborating

There are many ways to help your child find collaborators.

Invite friends to do project work with you. They might not have the same deep interest as your child — for them, it may be a simple one-time visit to the arboretum or the planetarium. Your child will still benefit from sharing the experience, seeing things from a friend's perspective, hearing another person's questions and seeing what they notice. Invite friends over when you do a special art activity — say, observing tree frogs and modeling them in clay. Again, for your child's friends, it may be a stand-alone experience, but your child will be able to combine his long-term study with the opportunity to work with others.

Consider starting a local project group. You can either invite others to study a topic in which your child has already expressed a strong interest or start a project group with other interested parents and choose a topic of general interest.

Start, help organize, or join an online project group. Share work online through photography sites and blogs. The children in the group can share their work with each other and e-mail or chat online

to share ideas, comments, and suggestions. This is also a great way to support and enhance a project group that can't get together frequently in person.

Start a project group as part of your local homeschool co-op. Find a core group of families willing to commit to a regular schedule of learning together. Do some initial education so everyone understands the goals of self-directed learning.

Create opportunities for special project-related activities that can be enjoyed by other children and their families (e.g., invite an ornithologist to give a free talk about birds at the library and invite other families) or take advantage of community events where your child can learn about project-related topics and share the experience with other children.

Keep in mind the benefits of mixed-age groups. Within reason, a range of ages can be much more effective than only same-age peers. (Just make sure your child isn't always the youngest or the oldest in every group.) Remember that siblings and family count. Inviting friends over to share ideas and construct something together can inject a project with new energy. Even if friends aren't working on the project as deeply as your child, your child still gets to share ideas, collaborate, learn to ask for help, learn to share, learn to offer help, explain things, learn to negotiate, learn to argue/make a case, etc.

things you might do

Siblings — Extended family — Neighbors — Friends

Homeschool co-op — Project groups — Online project groups

Copying/extending — Sharing ideas — Refining ideas

Supporting one another — Respecting diverse talents and skills

Discovering and sharing strengths, talents, interests, passions

Working together as a team — Shared responsibility

Handling disagreements — Negotiating — Articulating opinions

Communicating ideas, needs, thoughts — Asking for and offering help

Listening and speaking effectively — Learning to control emotions

Dividing work — Delegating — Leading — Offering suggestions

Connecting with Your Community

Encourage your child to talk to adults in the community about his project work and ask questions in person, by mail, or through e-mail.

Visit your local libraries, museums, universities, and special exhibitions related to your project. Take time to share what you are doing with the people around you: family members, friends, neighbors. You never know when someone might provide a great connection or idea for your child's project.

Encourage your child to write letters to individuals, companies, and/or organizations related to their project — e.g., write a letter to NASA for a space project or to a chef he watches on TV for a cooking project. Organizations will often send packets of interesting information to children who write letters. Have your child brainstorm about people or organizations to whom he could write. Encourage him to discuss his work. This is an excellent way to help your child explore his connection to the wider world. Projects give childen the opportunity to use their basic skills for a purpose. Written letters are a great way to practice writing skills, and children love to send and receive e-mail. Keep copies to help document the project.

Encourage your child to blog his project work and share it with friends and family.

Read the newspaper and look for local opportunities to mix project work with getting to know more about your community.

Talking with community members, your child can

- build his social skills,

- articulate ideas and questions,

- find and ask experts and mentors for help or guidance, and

- make relevant contributions to his community.

The most important thing is to listen to your child's ideas about connecting with your community. Pay attention and don't automatically dismiss anything. Write down every suggestion, even if you can't immediately see its potential. Get into the habit of journaling thoroughly — writing down as much as possible without filtering — so you can build a rich resource of potential ideas.

Help your child see how much his community offers him, and then help him explore how he might in turn help his community.

Have your child look for ways to make a significant contribution. He might do this by sharing his work with children and families he knows. He might build a blog or website. He might be able to make a concrete contribution to a specific place, such as making an information booklet about local plants or insects and distributing it at your local nature center or park. Your local library may have a bulletin board or display cabinet where he could share what he's learned with others. He might make a video and share it online. Ask your child, "How would you like to share this with other people?" Ask, "Could you use this to help someone else?"

things you might do

Librarians — Museum workers — Universities — Students

Community members — Business owners — Local organizations

Family — Friends — Church community — 4-H — Scouts

Talking with all sorts of people — Asking questions

Interviewing experts — Writing letters — E-mailing

Blogging — Online project groups — Websites — Wikis

Community events — Volunteer work — Park naturalists

Making and distributing booklets, brochures, field guides

Leading a workshop or one-time class for fellow homeschoolers

Preparing a display for your library, coffee shop, or other local business

As your child gets older, he should learn how to find or create his own community. He discovers what's already available in your area and how to make contact, join in, and see if it answers his needs. He learns how to find like-minded people online: virtual support groups, people with the same interests, people sharing their thoughts and their work. And if what he wants or needs isn't available, online or in real life, then he learns to initiate it. He forms a group, sends out some inquiring e-mails, teaches a class, starts a website, finds a mentor or becomes a leader. He makes it happen. He's learned the benefit of community; when he needs it or wants it, he can create it.

Reflecting

Reflecting is crucial for transforming a simple learning experience into a larger experience about learning how to learn.

In project-based homeschooling, we build reflection into the learning process. Rather than stopping with a finished product, we invoke that slow learning and build in an extra step, which sends us back to consider, refine, and revise our ideas and the work:

idea ⟶ work ⟶ representation ⟶ sharing ⟶
feedback ⟶ reflection ⟶ new ideas ⟶ more work ⟶
new representations ⟶ sharing what we've made with others

We create a feedback loop that raises the level of the work. But we're also looking beyond the work to the underlying thinking and learning strategies. It's thinking about thinking, learning about learning, solving problems about problem-solving.

Reflection is another part of the learning process that supports deep work and underscores its importance. Our environment, our

schedule, and now our way of talking about our work all send the same message: *This is important.*

Our concern goes beyond today's work to our long-term growth as thinkers, learners, problem-solvers, and makers.

We stop and talk about what we did, how we did it, and why. We discuss our goals, how we achieved them, what problems we had, and how we solved them.

We talk about cause and effect. We critique our work, think about the process, examine what happened, consider ways it could have been changed or improved, and look at what resulted from our choices. We see what we did and what happened as a result.

Then we have a chance to go back and tweak our final product or repeat our experience. There's no point in reflecting unless we have the time and the opportunity to go back and do something with our new insights, new questions, and new ideas.

We make today's experience larger and more important. What happened? What did we do? How did that work? We give ourselves feedback, and if we are working collaboratively, we give each other feedback. We stop and say, "What happened here? What's important? Do we want to do more? What will we do differently next time?"

When we build reflection into the learning process, we are digging beneath the ideas about the project to the underlying ideas about learning in general. We consider and discuss how we think, how we solve problems, how we approach new ideas, and so on. We revise and refine our ideas about how to learn.

We deepen the work by mining every bit of learning possible from it. We look at what's on stage — the work — and then we look behind the curtain at the process: how that work was created.

You model reflecting by adding this step to your mentoring. You take time to stop and review, look for possibilities, think about what you did and why, and consider what you might try in the future. You ask yourself the same questions that you encourage your child to ask herself:

- What did I accomplish?

- How did I do it?

- Did I do everything I could do? Could I do more?

- Is there anything I could do now to deepen or extend the work?

- Are there materials or tools that would help me do more?

- What would I change? What would I add?

- What would I do differently next time?

- What worked well? What didn't work well?

- Did I follow up on all my questions? my plans?

- Do I see any patterns or connections?

- Could I find ways to collaborate?

- Could I find ways to share?

Reflection is thinking about what we did, how we did it, and why we did it. We think about our goals, how we achieved them, what problems we had, and how we solved them.

We compare our outcome with what we wanted to achieve in the beginning. We examine the work we did and make sure we're satisfied with what we've accomplished.

Reflecting encourages you to appreciate your work and your achievements. You learn to see the possibility inherent in problems.

When we start our next project, we'll understand more — about ourselves, about the process of thinking and learning and problem-solving, and about how we make our ideas happen.

A Way to Live

Doing things that matter. Working on something real. This isn't just a way to learn — it's a way to live.

> "Creativity is sometimes associated with free expression, which is partly why some people worry about creativity in education. Critics think of children running wild and knocking down the furniture rather than getting on with serious work. Being creative does usually involve playing with ideas and having fun; enjoyment and imagination. But creativity is also about working in a highly focused way on ideas and projects, crafting them into their best forms and making critical judgments along the way about which work best and why." — Sir Ken Robinson, *Out of Our Minds: Learning to Be Creative*

Children, even when very young, have the capacity for inventive thought and decisive action. They have worthwhile ideas. They make perceptive connections. They're individuals from the start: a unique bundle of interests, talents, and preferences. They have something to contribute. They want to be a part of things.

It's up to us to give them the opportunity to express their creativity, explore widely, and connect with their own meaningful work.

Many parents and teachers agree readily that children have these abilities, but they want to believe they can (and perhaps should) blossom naturally with no interference from adults. Traditional educators think this will happen in the child's free time — presumably sometime between the school bell ringing in the afternoon and bedtime, in and amongst homework, extracurricular activities, team practices, and play dates. Many parents want to believe it will happen if their child has adequate free time. They hope their child will drift naturally away from the TV set and the video game console toward literature, nature, and science. They know that their child is intelligent and creative, and they expect — or hope — that deep thinking, rich exploration, and a strong work ethic will follow.

We can do better than that.

Rather than expecting children to seek out a balanced life all on their own, we can help them live it. We can create an everyday life that prioritizes what we value most. We can help our children grow up experiencing creativity, inquiry, and making ideas happen as part of their normal, everyday life, from their earliest days.

We can help them live a life based on learning and doing.

How to Finish

Many people can start a project; far fewer can follow it through to the end. Finishing is a skill in itself.

Acting as your child's learning mentor, you help curate his project. Questions, experiences, ideas, plans: you hold onto the individual threads of the project so your child can weave them into something meaningful. You help him maintain focus by continuing to shine a light on what matters, drawing him gently back, again and again, to his own deep interest.

And remember: *He decides what matters.*

You help him experience the beginning, the middle, and the end of a project:

- the initial questions and wonderings,

- the collecting of experiences and artifacts,

- the research and investigation and making of representations,

- the reflection and self-assessment, and

- the sharing with others.

As his mentor, you help him ask his own questions and judge his own work, and you help him decide when *he* is finished:

- Did you learn what you wanted to learn?

- Did you make what you wanted to make?

- Are you satisfied?

In the beginning, you help him figure out where his interests lie. You help him recognize and remember his own questions and plans.

In the middle, you help him build up the skills to do real work on things that matter to him. You help him make his ideas happen.

In the end, you help him accept his mistakes, work through problems, judge his own work according to his own standards, and determine whether he is satisfied and ready to move on.

Many adults, let alone children, stall in the information-gathering stage of a project. They keep collecting inspiration and ideas without ever moving forward to the point of making something of their own. Forget about finishing — they can't *start*.

In project work, you can't just keep taking things in — you have to put something out. You have to create, you have to build, you have to interpret. You have to share.

This is something that can become second nature if you live it every day, whether you are a child or an adult. If you become accustomed to creating and sharing, you are on the path of action. You aren't held back any longer by a fear of making mistakes or not measuring up. You are seeking answers to your own questions. You are creating and judging your own work. You are moving at your own pace. You are making your own decisions. The only thing that can stop you from achieving your goals is you.

Here's the thing about the advice in this book and all advice in general: You can read it and recognize its truthfulness without actually living it yourself. You can read good advice and compare it to what you already know and think ruefully, *Boy, is that true.*

But as solidly as good advice might land (it might even connect like a punch), you are unlikely to be able to transmit it to someone else with the same force.

Advice loses its power very quickly. You can try to pass good advice along to your own children — Do as I say, not as I do! — and they will hear "'blah blah blah I didn't but you should blah."

The best way to increase the odds that your child will live a certain way is to *live that way yourself*. The best way to raise readers is to read. The best way to raise doers is to do.

The best way to raise active, engaged learners is to be an active, engaged learner.

If you want to help your child learn how to finish — and it might be the most important lesson in this book — you must become a person who finishes.

Keys for finishing:

- Show up. Commit to making the time and using the time.

- Use small goals to accomplish big goals.

- Set yourself up to succeed: put a system in place.

- Aim for learned competence.

Show up. Commit to making the time and using the time. If you don't prioritize what is most important to you, it probably isn't going to happen. Just wishing and hoping won't make it so. Commit the time, the space, the materials, and the effort. Spend some time thinking about what kind of person you want to be and how you want to live. Think about your family culture. Does your daily life reflect your values? Think about your goals for your child. What kind of a thinker, learner, and doer do you want your child to be? Put these goals front and center and reflect on them often.

> How we spend our days is, of course, how we spend our
> lives. — Annie Dillard

Use small goals to accomplish big goals. If you don't set goals, you won't know how you're doing and you won't know when you're done. Project learning isn't about skimming around the surface of a subject — it's about digging deep. Encourage big ideas. Help your child determine what she wants to accomplish, and help her set some specific goals. Help her break those goals down into manageable tasks. Help her learn how to make a plan of action and then follow through. Help her keep track of her questions, plans, and intentions by posting them where you will see them every day. Enjoy small successes and celebrate problem-solving. Help her see how her efforts, over weeks and months, add up to achieving what she set out to do.

> Great things are not done by impulse, but by a series of small things brought together. — Vincent Van Gogh

Set yourself up to succeed: put a system in place. Don't leave it up to chance, mood, or whim. Build project time into your routine. Make it an important, permanent part of your schedule. Make your child's workspace clean, inviting, and attractive. Make sure he has the tools and materials he needs. Give his work regular attention and support, and make sure your family culture celebrates and values it. Give it a place of honor in your home and in your life. Reflect often on works-in-progress and help him turn ideas into goals into bite-size tasks. Make sure your workspace, your routine, and your family conversations reflect how much you value your child's work. Help him focus on what he cares about. Don't let it fall through the cracks. With a routine and a system in place, you'll be halfway to helping him succeed at what he wants to learn and do.

> We are what we repeatedly do. Excellence, then, is not an act, but a habit. — Aristotle

Aim for learned competence. Value effort over end results. Accept that people who do challenging work are always going to make mistakes along the way. Focus on nurturing the habits and attitudes that support strong thinking and learning. They are what will help your child succeed now and in the future. Your child should direct and manage his own learning, assess his own progress, and evaluate his own work. In life, he will often be in a situation where someone else is judging him, grading his work, giving him feedback. His project is his chance to take on this responsibility for himself. He measures his success against his own goals. He decides what to learn, how to learn it, and when he's done.

> If the bulk of your free time is spent watching other people do things, and little or no time is spent doing things yourself, it is impossible to grow smarter. —Jim Trelease

Rebooting a Stalled Project

Work has slowed. Your child is showing signs of boredom. She might be ready to move on, but you're not sure. Or, she still loves her project, but she hasn't done anything new for weeks.

Regular observation and journaling will help you recognize what's happening. You may notice your child is spinning her wheels and just repeating the same things over and over — staying in the same place, not making forward movement, not digging deeper. You may see that she's doing the same type of work over and over again in the same way. Things aren't changing and evolving. You need to help her develop her ideas further, work deeper, seek out more complexity.

Ways to jumpstart a stalled project:

- Tidy the studio/workspace — clean space attracts new work.

- Refresh resources — add new art or building materials.

- Bring in real artifacts your child can investigate and replicate.

- Invite friends over for new ideas, suggestions, sharing, extending.

- Mirror your child's work back to her — take photos and/or video, put work on display.

- Look through your journal for unanswered questions and plans.

- Pull out unfinished work and ask, "Are you done with this?"

- Ask if she wants to clean off the bulletin board and do something with the materials: make a scrapbook, portfolio, poster, book, journal, etc.

- Take a field trip. Repeat a field trip.

- Change perspective. Observe or draw something from above, below, inside, outside, close, far.

- Invite friends and family over to share what you've done so far.

- Revisit previous experiences. Redo previous activities.

- Clear out a large floor space and see what happens.

Help your child look for the places where she sees that she can improve, make something more clear or more complex, add more detail or new information. Ask, "Is there anything more you want to do with this?" Go through your journal and notes and remind her if she has unfinished plans. Say, "You said you wanted to paint this model. Do you want to do that?"

Always, your aim is to help your child learn to direct and manage her own learning. You want to encourage her project work without taking over. That light touch is a skill that takes time and experience. Give yourself time to learn how your child learns and how you can best support her. Give yourself the same support that you want to give your child.

Try to apply the least amount of interference necessary to keep things rolling. Respect your child's pace and keep in mind the natural ebb and flow of authentic intellectual work. But don't be so afraid of making a mistake that you don't interact at all. You're learning, too. You're learning how to mentor, encourage, facilitate, guide, support. You won't know where the line is if you don't accidentally cross it once in awhile. Be an interested, involved, and engaged co-learner and mentor. If you make mistakes, you'll know you're participating fully. And you'll know you're learning.

Wrapping Up a Project

The signs that a project is coming to a natural end are usually obvious. Your child has done a lot of work and now she's doing much less. Over time, her project-related play grew in complexity, but now she's playing less often and she's no longer adding anything new. She's happy with the work she's done and satisfied that she doesn't want to do anything else with it. She feels like she's accomplished what she set out to do.

She decides when she's done. Some children insist they're not finished with their project, ever, even when they're doing nothing new. Make sure she understands she can maintain her interest and keep studying her topic even while you start something new. She owns her interest. She feels it's a part of her, and her work becomes one of the ways she defines herself. Encourage that ownership.

She may be adamant about keeping her project because she feels she's discovered a lifelong interest. That's a wonderful thing you definitely want to support. But make sure she knows that she can start a new investigation without completely giving up her other interests. (This can especially happen with the first project, which often is about something that the child has always loved. They're afraid when you talk about the project being over, it means giving up that thing they love.) Make sure your child understands that the end of a project doesn't mean the end of enjoying that subject or even continuing to work on it. Many children, when asked what project they're working on, mention the thing they're doing now, then list every favorite project they've ever done. They want you to know they still care about those projects.

Your child may be reluctant to clean out his workspace and remove his representations to make way for something new. This is a time when high shelves come in handy. They're good for displaying items that he wants to honor and remember but doesn't need to work on every day. He may want to integrate some of his representations (e.g., costumes, props, clay figures) into his existing playthings so he can keep using them. Consider hanging a display of project-related work somewhere in your home, away from your child's daily workspace but in a place of honor. You're clearing the decks for new work, but you want to show that you still value what he's accomplished. Your family's treatment of his finished work should motivate him to keep learning and creating.

Make an event out of gathering, examining, and organizing the representations your child created and the artifacts you collected during the project. Take time to look at everything together and talk about each piece. Talk about what you can do with your child's project ephemera: make a book, scrapbook, portfolio, binder, or poster; fill a decorated box; make a website or video. Encourage him to dictate or write his memories about the project.

You may want to celebrate the culmination of a project by inviting family and friends over to see a display, exhibition, film, or show. Your child can make invitations, put up explanatory signs and posters, create brochures and schematic drawings — he could even make a map of the room identifying each thing he wants his guests to see. This is a great opportunity for him to explain his work, what he learned, and how he learned it. The process of deciding what to show and how to show it is a learning experience in and of itself. It is yet another opportunity for your child to teach someone else what he knows.

Older children and teens might like to create a website, a video, a book, or a series of podcasts. They might share what they've learned with younger children or peers through homeschooling groups, scouts, 4-H, schools, or daycares. They might display project documentation at your library, co-op, or church. Help them brainstorm ways to use their new knowledge to make something useful for others. Help them see that they can make a meaningful contribution to their community.

Your child has done a tremendous amount of work to reach this point. Celebrate it — and share it.

Clearing the Decks

It's time to get everything fresh, organized, and ready for the next project.

Do a deep clean of your workspace/studio. Sort through and discard or recycle the broken, dirty bits and the pieces that are too small to be used. Do this together. Discuss whether you want to reorganize or move anything and what you might want to add. During this process, your child will reacquaint herself with everything you have for making and creating; she'll get excited about using some of these materials again.

This is a great time to do a complex new art project or learn a new skill. Make paper from scratch. Learn to sew or weave. Carve stamps, learn to screen-print, or draw with charcoal. Become fluent in new materials and skills that your child can use in future representations. They will be valuable additions to her thinking and making vocabulary, giving her new ways in which to express her ideas.

During project work, your child will use whatever materials you have available to express her learning. If she's deep into learning about ocean life, she'll draw and paint fish, crabs, eels, shells. If clay is available, she'll sculpt in three dimensions. If she has large boxes, she might make a child-size fishing boat. If she has fabric, she might make nets and costumes. If floor space is available, she might create an entire dock scene and populate it with sea creatures and fish she's made.

The amount, variety, quality, and accessibility of materials you offer directly affects what she'll make, how she'll play, and how deeply she'll explore her interests. Her play and the representations she creates have a direct relationship with how much she learns and understands. Supply her with a rich storehouse of possibilities.

This is a great time to do those one-off activities and field trips you've been saving. Instead of distracting your child from her work, you're fueling new interests and giving her a well of experiences to draw from. Go out and explore the community. Do new things. Visit new places.

The richer her life experiences, the more likely she is to find exciting things to be curious about and the more likely she is to discover new talents and interests.

The Next Project

After a suitable break, it's time to choose the next project focus. Your child, now experienced with project work, might have her own idea about what she would like to study next. Still, keep documenting and keep looking for interests with potential. She may need your help to recognize an interest she hasn't yet identified.

As children get older and become more experienced with project work, they become adept at identifying interests that have rich potential for deep study. They know how they want to spend their dedicated project time. As they enter their teens, they may use this time to explore areas that could develop into serious hobbies or even a future career. If they plan to go to college, their project work can equip them with the thinking skills and learning habits they need for academic success — as well as help them be better prepared to choose a major.

The point of project-based homeschooling isn't only to become a skilled thinker and learner. It's just as important to find out what you're good at and what inspires you to work your hardest — so you can do as much of it as possible.

Older Children and Teens

As your child's learning mentor, your goal is to help him learn how to direct and manage his own learning.

As children get older, they require less and less from us as they pursue their own interests and projects. They seek more autonomy and more control. They are experienced at directing and managing their own learning. Still, your participation is essential.

At the beginning, your child provides the interest — but you may have to help him recognize it. As he becomes experienced at project learning, he will become adept at choosing the thing he wants to focus on next. He will know what it means to do long-term, meaningful investigation of something that matters to him, and he will choose those things that interest him the most.

He will recognize the value of the time you've set aside, the attention you bring, and the materials you provide. He will want to use these valuable resources to explore something truly important.

At the beginning, your child might need you to model how to wonder aloud, ask questions, consider alternatives. He looks to you as an example of how to approach learning as a researcher and investigator. As times goes on, this approach to learning becomes second nature to him. He is accustomed to asking questions, seeking out experts, collecting research materials, investigating first-hand, and creating original work. He looks automatically for ways to share what he learns with others.

At the beginning, your child will react to the environment that you create. The space you make becomes a self-fulfilling prophecy, encouraging the kind of work you want him to do: thoughtful, deliberate, multidimensional, layered, complex. In time, he will begin to request any necessary changes to his environment. He will ask for a film-maker's studio, a comic artist's workshop, a biologist's lab, a writer's study. He'll create the environment that supports the work he wants to do.

At the beginning, you will not only be your child's trusted resource but also his first and most important collaborator. He will look to you to set the tone, get the ball rolling, and keep it rolling. In time, he will take over. He knows what to do and how to do it.

He knows what to expect from the process, and he has a firm goal in mind.

But he will still need you to be that trusted resource. He will still need you as his first audience, his best collaborator, and his mentor. He will still need the support of a family culture that celebrates and supports meaningful work.

There are times when he might get off course, lose steam, hit a dead end. He will benefit from your input and suggestions.

As he takes on more responsibility, he will make more mistakes. You will reiterate the lessons of brainstorming and resilience. As he progresses, he will naturally work at his challenge level: the outer edge of his capabilities. That is the ideal place for him to be as a learner. Eventually he will reach independence and be completely in charge of his own life and his own decisions. Right now is your chance to support him as he practices all the skills, habits, attitudes, emotions, thinking, and learning that will eventually serve him well as an adult.

Mentoring self-directed learners is like rolling a hoop down a hill. You want to let the hoop roll on its own, only touching it when necessary to keep it upright and rolling, and even then as lightly as possible. As your child gets older, you should still pay attention to his work. He may not always articulate what he needs — you may see it before he does. He'll need your encouragement, your humor, and your support. He will continue to respond to your quiet attention and focus. Whatever you pay attention to will affect his efforts. Be sure to put your attention on what matters.

Hopefully, we start this process early — when our children are barely more than toddlers. We begin to introduce the core ideas of independence, responsibility, choice, personal passions, big ideas.

As our children get older, we want them to become project-oriented, self-directed learners, diving into each new interest with confidence and growing skill.

But you can make room for self-directed learning no matter how old your child is. You can change your life to reflect your true values and priorities. You can build new habits. You can choose where to put your attention and your effort.

All children need time in their learning life to focus on what matters most to them. For small children, it shows them why all learning is necessary: so they can do interesting things they care about. For teens, it is an essential discovery and development of their passions and talents. No matter what their age, it is the way children develop and strengthen their thinking skills, and it's the how they begin to take charge of their own learning.

Project-Oriented: The Relentless Learner

The goal of project-based homeschooling is to support your child so he can direct and manage his own learning. The focus is on his interests and his ideas. You create an environment and provide the tools, materials, and support he needs to make his ideas happen.

You help your child do the work he already wants to do. He chooses, directs, and manages his own learning, and you support and mentor him. The topic is his, the path is his, the decisions are his.

Rather than focusing on what particular facts and skills will be acquired, you make it possible for your child to develop strong thinking and learning habits. He acquires facts and skills organically while digging deeply into something that interests him.

Carrying out a complex, long-term project, your child becomes progressively more skilled in setting goals and making decisions. He begins to approach new interests and challenges in a project-oriented way. When faced with something he wants to know more about, he researches, investigates, and gathers materials. He reaches confidently for resources to learn what he wants to know. He makes representations. He contacts experts and knowledge gatekeepers. He communicates meaningfully with other people about his questions, his goals, and his plans. He actively engages with whatever interests him. He doesn't just passively consume; he creates, makes, and builds. He talks with other makers and builders. He is part of a community of thinkers and doers.

The child who has successfully negotiated a long-term, self-managed learning project will attack his next interest with confidence. He is building habits of mind that will serve him well for the rest of his life. And he's not done yet — he'll continue to hone those skills and add to them. He's finding out that skills are really useful, because they *help you do the things you want to do.*

The project-oriented child not only knows the process — he *demands* the process. He has taken ownership of his own learning. He is self-motivated because he chooses the work. It means something to him. He sets the goals. He decides what to do and how to do it. He owns the process and the result.

When the project-oriented child gets stuck, makes a mistake, or gets mired in confusion, he doesn't give up. He knows mistakes are an unavoidable part of learning. He brainstorms. He tries something new. He looks for an expert or finds a competent peer or adult to ask for help. He is intellectually engaged by solving problems. He sees himself as capable, resourceful, and able to deal with problems.

The project-oriented child seeks out meaningful work. He knows his interests and his questions can be explored deeply. He knows the joy of working hard on something that matters.

When you devote some of your learning time to helping your child pursue his self-chosen work, you help him become project-oriented. You help him become deeply acquainted with his passions, his talents, his interests. You help him find out what he can do with those interests.

You support your child's pursuit of his own self-chosen work, and you equip him with the thinking and learning tools he needs to succeed. You create a system that promotes meaningful work and the means to achieve it.

This is not a one-off experience. It is a way of thinking, learning, working, and sharing. It is a way of living.

Authenticity

This approach doesn't work if it isn't authentic. Your values have to match how you really live. Whatever you think is important for your child should be reflected in your own life and your own choices.

Your core values must align with your goals, which must align in turn with your everyday choices.

Really listen to what adults around you say about children — not their own children, but children in general. Many adults think very little of children and their abilities and motives — possibly because they think very little of themselves and their own abilities and motives. They transfer their negative beliefs onto children. If adults thought of themselves as strong, capable learners who enjoy challenges and want to contribute, presumably they would see children the same way.

> Watch your thoughts; they become words. Watch your words; they become actions. Watch your actions; they become habits. Watch your habits; they become your character. Watch your character; it becomes your destiny.
>
> — Frank Outlaw

Start with your thoughts. Do you believe your child is strong and capable? Do you believe she deserves time and support to explore her interests deeply? Do you want her to be able to work independently?

Pay attention to your words. Watch what you say to and about your child. Make sure your family culture reflects your values and goals. Your words express your beliefs. Make sure your child hears what you want her to hear.

Turn your words into actions. Make your environment support your goals. If you want your child to be able to work independently, make sure your environment, your routine, and your rules make that possible. Dedicate time to the things that are most important to you. Give your child time to work on the things that are most important to her. Pay the most attention to what matters most to you. Listen. Reflect. Model. Set good examples. Follow through.

Build habits that support the life you want to live. Choose one thing at a time to focus on, then commit to making it happen. Remind yourself of your goals every day. Turn today into a blueprint for your future.

Prioritize your character, your child's character, and your family culture. Think hard about what kind of person you want to be. Invest time and energy in exploring your own talents and interests. Make sure you live the life you want for your child. Find ways to connect with your community and make meaningful contributions. Think, learn, make, and do.

Find your meaningful work and do as much of it as possible. Let that be your destiny.

Keep in mind always the present you are constructing.
It should be the future you want.
Alicc Walker

About the Author

Lori Pickert and her family began homeschooling when her sons were four and seven. Before homeschooling, she founded a small private school with a Reggio-inspired, art- and project-based curriculum and served as director for several years. She has traveled the country speaking at conferences and leading workshops as a learning consultant. She writes about learning and mentors homeschooling families at Project-Based-Homeschooling.com.

Look for these forthcoming books:

Project-Based Homeschooling: Parent Handbook & Idea Book

Authentic Art for Young Children

How to Start

Visit our website:

You can find additional resources and community support at

Project-Based-Homeschooling.com

Project-Based-Homeschooling.com

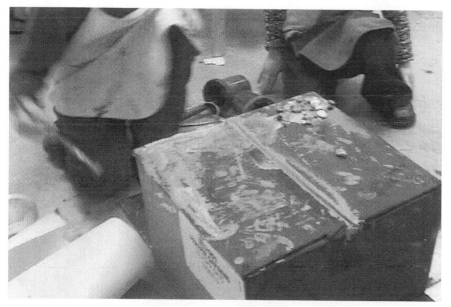

Make Something Cool

Stocking Your Studio
or Workspace

scissors + hole-punch + pencil sharpener + ruler = TOOLS
pencils = regular, colored & watercolor
pens = blue + black + colored ones, who knows?
markers = colored ones + black = thin + fat
chalk and oil pastels and charcoal sticks or pencils
watercolors = the kind that look shiny
tempera paint = white, black, yellow, red, blue =
  mix your own special colors, don't be lazy!
paper of all kinds + all sizes
paintbrushes = keep them clean!
leftover wrapping paper, newspaper, brown bags
glue & tape = lots and lots of TAPE
(there are a million kinds of tape)
(cellophane + masking + duct + foil + that sticky black one)
fabric = scraps + you can cut up old clothes!
yarn & string & twine = save everything!
wire = but be careful, it can be SHARP
buttons & sequins & puffballs & etc.
before you throw anything away, ask yourself:
  Could this be a robot's eyeball?
clean recyclables: cardboard boxes, tubes, lids & so on
leftover everything: tissue paper! ribbon! bread tabs!
plastic bottles, too = and plastic containers
have your mom or dad wash styrofoam meat trays (germy)
  — they're good for print-making
look at EVERYTHING and think:
         WHAT CAN I MAKE WITH THIS???

37117838R00102

Made in the USA
Charleston, SC
23 December 2014